Praise for *Miracle on Voodoo Mountain*

"I was privileged to volunteer at Respire and witness Megan's ministry. We support Respire, as Megan pours out her love and energy on the Haitian people, and encourage you to read this book."

—Laura Cassidy, MD and
Congressman Bill Cassidy

"Miracle on Voodoo Mountain is nothing short of amazing! Megan Boudreaux has done a great job of revealing not only her heart but also the work God is doing in Haiti. Be inspired to lend your support, still so desperately needed in Haiti, as you read about God's faithfulness and what He is doing at Respire."

—Adam Hayward,
NFL linebacker,
Washington Redskins

"I met Megan in Haiti the day after I met my little girl, Missy. And in retrospect our introduction was all part of God's sovereign plan—hearing her story and seeing her kids helped galvanize my resolve to hang in there through two years of adoption hurdles and finally bring my daughter home. Megan is beyond inspirational—she's more like a gasoline torch placed next to a pile of good intentions! She will ignite your heart to a bigger, riskier kind of love."

—Lisa Harper, author,
Bible teacher, and
Women of Faith® speaker

"Megan Boudreaux is a young lady who exemplifies Christ-likeness. In obedience to God's calling, she sacrificially put her life on hold and trusted God to use her to make a dramatic difference in the material and spiritual lives of hundreds of impoverished and enslaved Haitian children. *Miracle on Voodoo Mountain* is the inspiring and uplifting story of Megan's Spirit-driven calling and her bold action in response to that call."

—David Limbaugh,
author, *New York Times*
bestseller *Jesus on Trial*

"Without fearing the unknown, Megan obeyed the vision she received and was led to some of the world's most vulnerable children. This is a great story of not only God's provision but also courage when confronted by spiritual and political opposition. It is a testimony to the power of God and the significance of one person who will step out and respond with a yes to God's call. As Megan continues to respond to the needs that surround her, her story also shows us that lasting impact and change are the results of many people trusting Jesus, working together, praying, listening, loving, and partnering with the people they serve."

—JIM BEISE, FOUNDER,
LA FONDERIE, PARIS, FRANCE; AND
MISSION PASTOR, LA CROIX CHURCH

Miracle on
VOODOO
MOUNTAIN

Miracle on
VOODOO MOUNTAIN

A Young Woman's Remarkable Story of Pushing
Back the Darkness for the Children of Haiti

MEGAN BOUDREAUX

W PUBLISHING GROUP

AN IMPRINT OF THOMAS NELSON

Published in Nashville, Tennessee, by W Publishing Group, an imprint of Thomas Nelson.

Thomas Nelson titles may be purchased in bulk for educational, business, fund-raising, or sales promotional use. For information, please e-mail SpecialMarkets@ThomasNelson.com.

Unless otherwise noted, Scripture quotations are taken from the Holy Bible, New International Version®, NIV®. ©1973, 1978, 1984 by Biblica, Inc.™ Used by permission of Zondervan. All rights reserved worldwide.

Scripture quotations marked NLT are taken from *Holy Bible*, New Living Translation. © 1996. Used by permission of Tyndale House Publishers, Inc., Wheaton, Illinois 60189. All rights reserved.

Scripture quotation marked ESV are taken from the English Standard Version. © 2001 by Crossway Bibles, a division of Good News Publishers.

Library of Congress Cataloging-in-Publication Data

Boudreaux, Megan.
  Miracle on Voodoo Mountain : a young woman's remarkable story of pushing back the darkness for the children of Haiti / Megan Boudreaux.
      pages cm
  Includes bibliographical references.
  ISBN 978-0-529-11094-7 (hardcover)
  1. Church work with children—Haiti—Gressier. 2. Missions—Haiti—Gressier. 3. Boudreaux, Megan. 4. Christianity and other religions—Vodou. 5. Vodou—Relations—Christianity. I. Title.
  BV2616.B68 2015
  266'.0237307294—dc23

                        2014024082

Printed in the United States of America
15 16 17 18 19 RRD 5 4 3 2 1

*To my precious daughter, who started this all, Michaëlle,
and to the rest of my beautiful children, Jessica, Johanne,
and Saintil, who are all parts of this incredible story*

Contents

CONTENTS

Acknowledgments

I would love to express my gratefulness to the many people who have molded and shaped me into the young woman I am today, and who have also walked alongside me at different moments through this adventure here in Gressier.

First and foremost to Josh, my best friend, my encourager, my husband. I am blessed by your unending support, optimistic attitude, and willingness to watch the children during the long days of writing and editing. I could *not* have finished this without you. To Susy Flory, for taking the time to come to Gressier and see what God has done and for guiding me in this process. Thank you for believing in my story and in what God is doing on Bellevue Mountain. Debbie Wickwire and Lisa Harper, thank you for pursuing me, believing in me, and encouraging me to tell this story.

To Kate Hays, Mr. John, and Mrs. Diane Crews, thank you for bringing me on my first mission trip ever. My life was beginning to change with that, and I didn't even know it.

Thank you, Norris and Melissa. Without your support, encouragement, advice, and love, my family would not be as sane and Respire Haiti would definitely not be the same. Steve and Renee, thanks for giving us the best wedding and honeymoon advice. We love you guys dearly. Chris Hearp, thanks for listening to Melissa and coming to visit me when I showed you a piece of land that was just a big dream. To all at Haiti Serve, from the bottom of my heart, thank you for believing in the dream of a young, naïve girl.

Mr. John Paul Funes, as I teetered on the edge, you gave me just the right amount of push to let me go. Thank you for your belief in what God was starting. Sister Martha Ann Abshire, thank you so much for bringing me to Haiti for the first time and sharing your wisdom and experience with me.

Curt and Nancy Richardson, thank you for letting God use you both to catapult this amazing journey. You'll never really know how much you built. Harold Hanusch, "Tex," thank you for giving me my first iced coffee in Haiti ever. I am blessed by your support.

Gwen, Suzanne, Michelle, Jan, and the whole 147 Million Orphans team, you guys are inspiring. Thank you for bringing me Diet Coke, lots of laughs, and encouragement.

Amelia, Raffi, and Ritha Belizaire, thank you for sitting in the dark with me for hours. I'm in awe of your love for the Haitian people, and I am constantly encouraged by your family. Caroline Sada, you are an incredibly brave and wise woman; thanks for being such an encouragement and fighting for the Haitian people. The McKeehans and the Lecroys, thank you for being amazing advocates of freedom. It is a blessing to walk alongside you during this fight. Adam Hayward, thanks for visiting Gressier and believing in my vision. Thanks for playing in the NFL but remembering what God has ultimately called you to.

Bret Pinson, who would have known that the journey would look like this? Thank you for being a mentor, organizer, and believer in God's plan here in Gressier. Kathryn Davis, you are a rock star. I will never forget our many adventures and your worship, prayers, and encouragement. The hard days with Gabriel were made better by you. I love you! Jessi White Morris, thank you for giving so much of your life to come on this journey with me here in Gressier. Kyle Fishburn, thank you for believing in my dream enough to drop your life in California and come live in Haiti. For not giving up when things didn't always work out right and for never complaining about eating Haitian food every day. God has special plans for your life.

Our Haitian staff—Tachi, Darlene, Nedgi, Jackie, FiFi Wilbur, Mr. Colin, Mr. Gracia, Dieumaitre, Arnold, Patrick, Belo, Wadley, and so many more—Respire Haiti would not exist if it weren't for your incredible heart for the Lord and for Gressier. And thank you to our American staff (past and present), Sharon, Stephanie, Adam, Kameryn, Amber, Hannah, Samantha, Amanda, Jessi, Kat, and many more. I know there is no place you guys would rather be, and there's no place that I would rather you be too!

Bernard, where would I be without you? Thank you for being the fearless leader and translator that you are. God brought you to Gressier and to me for that reason. Rita and Dan Noel, thank you for going against the grain and bringing your life, skills, and joy to Gressier. Rita, you know how much I have appreciated your wisdom and encouragement.

Dad, I know you are looking down from heaven and smiling with joy at the freedom that is on Bellevue Mountain. To T-tone, thank you for walking me down the aisle, even if that meant coming all the way to Haiti to do it. I love you more than words.

Lindsey, my sister, no matter the miles, no matter the time apart, you will always be the most incredible big sister. I love you. Zack, thank you for only being a phone call away and for telling me to always wear gloves.

And to the rest of my family, Aunt Chris, Uncle Butch, Nanny, Uncle Doug, Aunt Michelle, Uncle Jerry, Aunt Kathy, Aunt Tina, Kellie, Amy (and our car Amy-Lou), Caleb, Stacey, Terry, Joey, Brittany, Laura, Jack, Molly—and of course the one who is responsible for all of us being on this earth, MawMaw. I know you are looking down from heaven and laughing at my stubbornness. I'm glad it's genetic.

And last but definitely not least, thank you, Mom. What can I say? You have believed in me my whole life, and you loved me enough to let me go so I could spread my wings and be a mom to so many others. You've given the greatest gift of all, sharing me with Gressier and these children.

The Dream Tree

And all the trees of the field shall clap their hands.
—Isaiah 55:12 ESV

It was like a recurring nightmare, but I wasn't exactly scared. It was more like a shot of adrenaline when I saw the leafy green tree, and I'd wake in a bit of a panic, wondering why I couldn't get it out of my mind. I always woke up immediately after I saw the tree in my dream, my eyes open and heart thumping. I'd only seen it once, on the top of a mountain in Haiti more than a thousand miles away from my apartment in Louisiana.

I worked in marketing for a hospital in Louisiana called Our Lady of the Lake, and I had been sent on a business trip to a medical clinic in Haiti in August 2010, just months after the massive earthquake that left the capital of Port-au-Prince and other surrounding cities in ruins. This was my second trip to Haiti, and I was overwhelmed by the devastation and despair.

On the last day of my trip, a few new friends and I fled the chaos of the capital and headed west to the gorgeous mountains of Gressier (pronounced *gray-see-ay*). The fresh air and warm sunshine beckoned, and we walked through the village and climbed up a rocky trail onto Bellevue Mountain. After making our way through some thick green bushes, we came out on top in a field of lush green grass.

With my 360-degree view, I felt tiny under the overarching dome of the summer sky. In front of me was the bright blue of the Caribbean. I turned around, breathing in the fresh air and enjoying the feel of the breeze blowing through my hair and cooling the back of my neck. Behind me were mountains covered in thick green vegetation, like something out of *Jurassic Park*. My eyes followed valleys that disappeared into shadows, reddish-brown paths that cut through the jungle, and wisps of smoke curling up here and there.

Then details started to come into focus, and I saw tents peeking up everywhere in the distance. Some were earthquake relief tents, pale gray and marked USAID. Others were hastily made of colored tarps. I started to pick out people moving around, walking along paths or working in their yards. Down in the valley I saw some children carrying heavy jugs of water on their heads. I watched as they walked what seemed like miles.

We grew hot out in the sun and headed toward the only bit of shade on the mountain—a lone tamarind tree next to the path. The grayish-brown trunk looked thin and frail but somehow became bigger and more substantial when we got close. The canopy was thick and heavy and bright green with feathery leaves. From a distance it looked like a giant fern plopped on top of a big stick. We took refuge underneath as I thought about all of the people I'd seen. Most were hungry, many were sick, and everyone was still traumatized by the earthquake.

Remembering the hungry-looking children I had seen hauling water, I thought, *Someone needs to come here.*

Never in my wildest dreams did I imagine that someone would be me. But as soon as I got back home to Louisiana, the dreams started. They weren't about the women I'd seen or the raggedy children or the dusty tents—just the tree. I longed to see it again and felt as though it was calling me back to Haiti, as if my spirit was being lured.

After a couple of months of these dreams, I decided to tell my boss, John Paul Funes, what was going on. I'd only been working at the hospital for ten months at the time, and I thought it was my perfect job. I loved my coworkers and my boss, and I enjoyed my work helping plan special events. So I knocked on his door, anxious and hesitant, and I heard his jovial, "Come on in!" I perched on the edge of a chair and began rambling about Haiti, trying to explain the people and the children and my dreams of the tree.

John Paul looked up in the middle of my rambling, smiled a calm, relaxed smile, and said, "If you think God is calling you to Haiti, you absolutely need to go."

That wasn't what I expected to hear. What kind of person would encourage a twenty-four-year-old city girl who loved to go shopping and wear cute outfits to just pick up and move to a hot, poverty-stricken country like Haiti? But he did. "Go ahead and try it," he added. "If it doesn't work out, there will always be a place for you here."

So I went.

It's been three years now, and so much has changed. When I showed a picture of the cover of this book to my ten-year-old,

Haitian-born daughter, she immediately recognized the tree and the silhouettes of mother and daughter.

"I'm in your story?" she asked, eyes wide with wonder and delight.

I looked at her with tears in my eyes. *Sweet girl, you* are *the story*. But I didn't say it out loud to her. Not yet.

This is our story, how we met underneath the tamarind tree and how she changed my life forever.

ONE

Okay, God, I'm Here

Courage is fear holding on a minute longer.
—George Patton

Exhausted and as clean as I could get with a bucket of cold water, I untangled my mosquito net, draped it over the bed, tucked the ends underneath the mattress, and crawled in. It was pitch-black, but I looked up anyway toward the mosquitoes buzzing around. Slowly, the frenzied whine of their tiny wings was drowned out by a different sound.

Thump, thump, thump.

I listened.

Thump, thump, thump.

Voodoo drums.[1] My ears vibrated with the sound as my heart began to beat inside my chest to the rhythm. I wrestled the mosquito net away and got up to lock my bedroom door. Then I reached for my Bible and my little flashlight. I began praying over my bed, actually praying over everything, trying to calm my beating heart as my first day as a resident of Gressier, Haiti, came to an end.

When I'd stepped off the plane in Port-au-Prince that

morning—January 9, 2011—the only information I had was the name of my driver, along with a small piece of paper with my new address scribbled on it. The driver was a polite local man who led me to a beat-up Nissan Patrol. I watched anxiously as he threw my bags in the bed of the truck, covered them with a tarp, and tied everything down tightly with ropes. I felt as though I could barely breathe. *What am I doing here?* kept running through my mind like an endless repeating chorus.

I had no idea how long it would take to get to my new home in Gressier, just twenty miles from the airport. As we drove, I saw clusters of tents, piles of trash, and chaos everywhere. The humid air was heavy on my skin, and I smelled sewage through the open window. I'd already been to Haiti twice, but this time things seemed worse than on my previous visits. The sweat began to bead up on my lip as we dodged motorcycles, trucks, cars, and children. The ride was silent, except for the thousands of people we passed who were screaming at me with their eyes.

Two hours later we stopped next to a large, bent, black wire gate. I looked at my driver and smiled timidly; he looked back at me with his eyebrows scrunched up and mouth tense. *Is he worried about something?*

After he handed me my bags, I thanked him, paid him in American dollars, and turned around. Behind me, I heard his gentle voice say in his lilting accent, "Call me if you need a ride back to the airport." He handed me a business card. It read "Moliere. Private Taxi Driver." I took it and tried to smile, but I'm not sure I succeeded.

I stood in front of the gate. *I can't believe I'm finally here.*

Although I wasn't certain of much, I was sure God had been calling me to move to Gressier, a suburb of Port-au-Prince and the town I had visited five months earlier. On that trip I'd met a Haitian friend named Bernard, who acted as my translator. Bernard searched for months to find a house I could rent, but houses were hard to find because almost one year before—January 12, 2010—most of the buildings in Gressier had crumbled to the ground in the giant earthquake that destroyed much of the country. The epicenter was just west of where I stood.

The earthquake had measured 7.0 on the Richter magnitude scale. This was not as strong as some of the most destructive earthquakes in other places, but the Haiti earthquake occurred very close to the surface. Because of poor building-construction practices and other problems, more than 250,000 people were killed and 1.5 million people displaced. Nearly every person in Haiti lost a family member or friend, and while most of the bodies had been removed, the destroyed houses were still there, sad piles of gray rubble. Ninety percent of the rubble had yet to be cleared, and some 800,000 people were still living in a thousand camps around the capital.[2]

Bernard kept sending me e-mail updates on the fruitless search for a rental. *No luck. Sorry.*

Finally Bernard called, distress in his voice. "I just visited the last place I know of in Gressier," he said. "Nothing."

I didn't understand. "I'm sure God wants me in Gressier," I said slowly. I thought of the tree from my dream and the tugging on my heart. "Maybe you can try the next town over?"

Bernard agreed to continue the search, and we hung up. I dropped to my knees, scared and unsure. I was twenty-four years old, I'd just quit my job and sold almost everything, and I felt I'd been listening to God's voice as I never had before. I was being obedient. *So why isn't there a place for me to live?*

God's gentle reminder came, a whisper deep in my heart. *Trust*. Just one word. *Trust*. I took a deep breath and let it out in a deep sigh. A few minutes later my phone rang again, Bernard's name flashing on the screen. I hit Talk, and his voice burst out of the phone, excited.

"Hey, Megan. The same lady I just visited called back and said you can stay at her house. She's not using the inside of her house." He explained that the woman and her family camped out in the front yard. So many people died in the earthquake that, like many others, they were afraid to sleep inside and felt safer in a makeshift tent, often just a plastic tarp or a sheet of rusty tin held up by sticks.

As Moliere drove away, I pushed open the black metal gate to my new front yard and whispered to myself, "This is my new home," although I couldn't quite believe it yet. I was greeted by a few chickens wandering around pecking at the dirt, a boiling pot of something over a little charcoal fire, and many kisses on my cheek from a mother and her two grown children who lived in the front yard. Bernard had told me that a nineteen-year-old boy named David lived upstairs on the flat roof, but the inside of the house was empty. Before I arrived, the tent family had asked if they should leave, but I told Bernard to tell them it was okay to stay. I didn't want them not to have anywhere to go.

My new house was made out of rough, gray concrete blocks, the walls painted a sickly green inside. As the family led me through the heavy metal front door, I got a few instructions in broken English and many hand gestures. I put my bags down in my bedroom while they motioned for me to come into the bathroom. I followed and, out of habit, flipped on the light switch. Nothing. My new friends chuckled. *I get it. No electricity.*

One of the women, named Say Say, motioned to an empty paint bucket and then took my hand, pulling me gently outside to a private cistern where I would have to fetch water. *Okay, no electricity and no running water.* I smiled a bit. *This is going to be interesting.*

"Mesi!" I thanked them with one of the few Haitian Creole words I knew. They smiled and left me inside, alone.

It was getting dark, so I figured I should take a shower before I had no light at all. I grabbed the five-gallon paint bucket from the bathroom and carried it outside. Next to the cistern was a smaller bucket tied to a rope. I threw it in, dragged it sideways to let it sink and fill with water, then pulled it up and dumped the water in my paint bucket. I hauled the little bucket up several times until mine was full, then picked it up. *Who knew water could be so heavy?* I listened to the precious water slosh around inside the bucket as I awkwardly carried my bathwater back inside, stopping several times from the weight.

Inside the bathroom I propped up the tiny flashlight I'd brought, and as I splashed the first plastic cup of water on my skin, the freezing cold shock of it took my breath away. I let out a small yelp. *I'm actually going to have a heart attack from this water, and someone will find me naked and dead from cold water shock in this bathroom.*

As I shivered, I laughed, and after splashing a second cup full, I prayed out loud. "God, thanks for not bringing me to Gressier just to die of shock during a freezing cold bath." This began the first of many freezing flashlight showers. I remembered how heavy the bucket was and tried to use as few cups as possible.

Exhausted, I gobbled down an energy bar and finally fell asleep, my Bible on my chest inside the mosquito net. Every so often a rooster crowed, and in the background the voodoo drums vibrated through the night in the thick, heavy darkness.

It seemed as if it were just a few minutes later when I heard goats bleating, chickens cackling, pigs grunting, and people talking. I looked at my watch: 4:57 a.m. *Ridiculously early.* I turned over and tried to ignore the noise outside, but it didn't work. I was going to have to face the day. I gave up on sleep and climbed out of bed. I wanted to see where the noise was coming from, so I climbed the stairs to the roof.

The roof was flat, gray concrete with rusted metal bars sticking up randomly throughout. Right outside the door to the stairs was David's red-and-gray camping tent where he slept every night. I walked to the middle of the roof. Behind me was a hill covered with bushes and vines. Right next to the house, overhanging part of the roof, was a beautiful green mango tree with big, luxurious leaves. On the other side was a smaller tree full of big bunches of curvy green bananas, all growing upward. I knew they were actually plantains; on a previous trip I had eaten some tasty little cakes made with the starchy fruit. The lush green vegetation all around me contrasted sharply with the gray concrete blockhouses and the dusty brown dirt road in front of the house that slouched down toward the highway below.

I stood and watched as the neighborhood woke up. A line of small children filled their buckets at a community water pump right outside my new front gate. Women worked on their houses or swept around their tents. A man across the street chopped at some bushes with a big machete. A small corner store was selling what looked like soap, oil, and rice. I didn't have a plan, and since I was unsure what to do next, I went downstairs to the front-yard tent and smiled at my new, and only, friends.

"Bonjou," I offered.

They smiled back. Realizing I couldn't say a word of Haitian Creole or understand a word other than hello or thank you, I waved and went back inside.

I need to do something. I have never been good at relaxing or sitting still, so I unpacked my things, organized my bedroom, and went back up to the roof. The air was fresher up there. I gazed beyond the houses to the right, to the mysterious dark-green mountains behind. I saw threads of gray smoke curling upward from dozens of cooking fires where people lived, tucked away in the valleys and hollows. *Is that where the drumming came from?*

My eyes wandered back, following a ridge down to a flat green mountain above the neighborhood and directly across from the spot where I was standing. *Is that Bellevue Mountain?* I heard a rustling sound and looked down. A little girl was sorting through some dry beans next to a small charcoal stove in the yard next door; I smiled and waved and she waved back. I felt restless and had nothing else to do, so I walked downstairs again and prayed.

"Okay, God, I'm here. What do I do?" *Crickets.* I got nothing.

Okay, God. But I can't just sit here and eat energy bars forever. I know I'm here for a reason, right? Please show me why.

TWO

Throwing Rocks at Birds

Dèyè mòn gen mòn.
Behind the mountain, there are mountains.
—A Haitian proverb

The next day, whenever I was quiet, my fear rose up again as it had during the previous night when I'd heard the voodoo drums in the dark. So I tried to stay busy: I prayed and wrote in my journal, and I kept watching the neighborhood from the roof. I felt as though I was waiting, but for what?

As I sat on the roof and watched the sun go down on my second day in Haiti, I ate another energy bar for dinner. I felt so very alone. *Am I crazy? My friends are right. I must be crazy to leave such a great life in the States for a place like this. I don't even know why I'm here. Oh Lord. Did I make a mistake? Should I just go back home?*

I needed to hear a familiar voice that night, so I made a quick decision to splurge on an expensive two-minute cell phone call to my mom. As soon as I heard her voice, the tears began to well up in my eyes.

"I'm fine, Mom." I tried hard to keep my voice steady and to sound sure of myself even though I wasn't. "It's beautiful here." As I got off the phone I repeated the same routine as the night before, except this time my sobs and sniffles drowned out the beating drums in the distance as I cried myself to sleep.

I awoke the next day to the same goat-chicken-pig-people sounds and knew if I stayed around the house again all day, I would implode with fear and anxiety. I ate my breakfast energy bar, dried up my tears, and looked at David, the roof boy. We traded smiles, and I asked, "Bellevue Mountain?"

He said something in Creole and looked at me, eyes wide. *Okay, he doesn't understand.*

I pointed to myself, then moved two fingers like legs walking uphill and pointed toward the front of the house to show him I wanted to walk to Bellevue Mountain. It was the only place I had a name for in Gressier, and since I had holed myself up in the house for two days, I thought it would be refreshing to get out.

"Okay," David said with a smile. *He got it!* I smiled, too, with a little jolt of happiness at having a plan, if only a small one. I ran down the stairs ahead of David and waved at Say Say and her family on the way out. David wrenched open the gate, and we pushed through a herd of goats nibbling on weeds by the side of the road.

Tons of children waited for their turn at the community water pump right outside of my gate. I looked at my feet as we walked, avoiding the gaze of dozens of dark brown eyes on me. As we strolled down the street, people yelled at me in Creole, and children ran up and grabbed my hands and clothes. David answered them back, his voice firm. Whatever he said made them laugh and stop touching me.

I followed close behind as he led me down the uneven brown road. We stepped onto a narrow footpath with clumps of weeds and bushes dotting the sides. We walked through a group of long-horned cows with tiny ropes around their necks, grazing peacefully. The path wound between a few decrepit houses and down into a small valley through a leafy green mango grove where the soil was rich and dark. As the path began to curve upward, we climbed a steep hill and came through some bushes to the top. It was flat and green, and my eyes followed the path that cut through the grass until I saw it. There, just as I remembered, stood the tamarind tree. It was a rich dark green, about twenty feet tall, with a single sturdy trunk and strong, supple branches that curved gracefully down at the ends.

I waved toward the tree and the land around it and asked, "Bellevue Mountain?"

"*Wi.*"

I had chills. It was the same tree I'd stood under five months ago, the tree that kept appearing in my dreams. I was actually here, standing in the same place where I'd first heard the sweet whisper of my Father.

The top of Bellevue Mountain is a beautiful place. A cow relaxed nearby on the lush green grass, and I could see beyond the edge of the mountain all the way out to the turquoise sea. I smiled and took a deep breath, staring off into the distance.

A movement caught my eye, and that's when I first saw her—a little girl, maybe six or seven years old. She was wearing a raggedy, soiled, yellow tank top that was too big, hanging off one shoulder down to her thin elbow. It must have been a woman's shirt, and she wore it as a dress.

She was barefoot with matted orange hair, and her bony figure screamed of malnutrition. I watched as she threw a rock at a blackbird.

11

I felt drawn to her. She was so little. *What is she doing out here all alone?* I remembered the girls I'd seen earlier that morning, walking to school. They each wore a uniform with their hair neatly braided and tied with bright ribbons. *Why isn't she in school?*

The bird jumped up and flew a few feet away, and the little girl followed. She threw another rock.

I got close enough to call out, "What are you doing?" I was sure she didn't understand me, so I glanced at David, and he repeated my question in Creole. His English wasn't great, and I hoped he could figure out what I was saying.

The little girl answered back in Creole. "There are two blackbirds." David turned toward me to translate, then turned back around and pointed to the birds in the sky overhead to make sure I understood.

"Yes, I see them. But what are you doing?" I asked again.

As she rocketed off in Creole, I received another loose translation from David. "Throwing rocks at birds."

"Yes, I see. But why?"

Her beautiful brown eyes widened as she looked up at me. "To eat!" She turned around and threw more rocks. A little boy I hadn't noticed before approached and tugged on my arm. He looked up at me and whispered with a grin as David translated. "It's true. She eats birds."

All of a sudden I got it: she was hungry, so she was trying to kill a bird.

She kept throwing rocks at the birds, and when she finally got tired, she came closer. I tried to find out her name, her age, and where she lived, but David's translation skills weren't quite enough. We all laughed a little.

Bernard arrived shortly after to help with translation; David had called him when we left the house. Bernard was fluent in Haitian Creole and English, which he'd learned from a group of deportees from Brooklyn.

A few moments later I saw an older woman walking up the mountain toward us. She spoke broken English and told me the little girl's name was Michaëlle *(Mick-kay-ell)*. Then, in an emotionless voice, she explained, "Mother dead. No father. Nobody wants her." She looked at me, then turned to Bernard and began explaining in Creole that no one wanted Michaëlle, so she had taken her in. She called herself Michaëlle's aunt, even though they weren't related.

In that moment my heart broke. I wanted to press my hands over Michaëlle's ears so she couldn't hear what this woman said. I wanted to tell her, "It's not true! You are loved and wanted and special!" But I noticed that Michaëlle didn't even flinch at the harsh words. She must have heard them before. Tears came to my eyes, and my chest grew tight as the reality hit me that this little raggedy girl was all alone in the world. *I can't even imagine what you have been through,* I wanted to tell her. But I couldn't.

The woman continued, telling Bernard her house had been destroyed in the earthquake and she'd moved from outside of Port-au-Prince to Gressier several months ago. "No one wanted Michaëlle, so I brought her here although I can hardly afford to feed her." Bernard looked at me, his eyes sad as he translated.

"Does Michaëlle go to school?" I asked.

"No, she can't go to school. No money," she said.

I remembered hearing about Haitian schools. Private schools were available, but only the wealthier children could go there. Public schools cost money, too, for registration, books, paper and pencils, and uniforms. For many people, struggling just to get enough food to stay alive, $150 a year for school was far out of their reach.

Then the woman said something that surprised me. "I have four other children staying with me. They go to school, and that's all I can afford."

My chest tightened as I pictured everyone in Michaëlle's house waking up for the day, getting ready to go to school, and only Michaëlle left behind. I could imagine her sitting alone, believing no one wanted her and that she wasn't worthy to go to school. Impulsively I looked straight at Michaëlle, tuning out the old woman, and asked in a loud, clear voice, "Do you want to go to school?" Her eyes got big and shot over to Bernard. She could tell I was asking her a serious, yet exciting, question. In a quietly intense voice Bernard repeated my question to her in Creole.

"Yes! I would love to," she said and quickly hugged us both. With Bernard's help I made arrangements with the woman to meet again the next day to get the little girl's information. Then I looked back at Michaëlle with a big smile.

"Okay. Let's go tomorrow to enroll you in school." Michaëlle began jumping up and down. I was excited too. I'd been waiting for something to happen, and now I had a clear task before me.

I went to sleep that night and again heard the voodoo drums. Putting my earplugs deep inside my ears, I lay still, looking up at the ceiling.

Thump, thump, thump.

I squirmed in my bed, trying to drown out the sound.

Thump, thump, thump.

As I stilled my body, it felt as if my heart began beating to the drums. Anxious, scared, and unsure, I began praying out loud and eventually dozed off to sleep.

Early the next day I found the path and climbed Bellevue Mountain again, following the woman's instructions to find Michaëlle in a big blue tent on the side of the mountain with the older woman, four other children, and several adults. The relationship this mishmash family shared was unclear and unsettling.

Michaëlle was playing in front of the tent in the same ragged yellow dress she had worn the day before. When she saw me, she ran inside and changed into a blue-and-white princess dress costume with white shoes and ankle socks. Her excitement propelled her ahead of me down the path. I had to walk fast to keep up with her. As I followed her down the mountain, I wondered who she was and why she was living in such a strange situation. *Is it because of the earthquake? How did her mom pass away? Why was she trying to eat a bird? Was she really that hungry? Why isn't she being fed? And why was she wearing that old yellow rag when she had a cute dress to wear?* I had lots of questions, and I wanted some answers.

But first, I needed to follow Michaëlle down the mountain. I didn't know then that Michaëlle was not just leading me down Bellevue Mountain but into a whole new purpose for my life. I didn't know that this hungry orphan girl wasn't just living in a foster home in that blue tent; she worked there. And instead of going to school, she hauled water, scrubbed dirty dishes, swept the floor, washed clothes, and, exhausted at the end of the day, slept on a piece of cardboard under the table. She worked sick or well, fed or hungry, rain or shine. Michaëlle had no one to watch out for her, care for her, or make sure she got an education. At only seven years old she was alone, unvalued, and forgotten.

But I didn't yet know this. All I knew was I needed to run to catch up. The waiting was over, and there was work to be done.

THREE

Prom Queen Meets Roaches

You must do the things you think you cannot do.
—Eleanor Roosevelt

The bench creaked as I tucked my head as far between my knees as I possibly could and contorted my seven-year-old body into a tiny ball. I was a hot, sticky mess in the Louisiana heat, but I didn't care. I felt a little safer as I clutched my knees and tried to shove my head down even farther.

It was the day of my father's funeral, and I'd bravely walked in with my ten-year-old brother, Zack, and my nine-year-old sister, Lindsey. But somehow I got lost in the shuffle, and that's when I found the bench. I was trying so hard to disappear. When I realized I couldn't, I began listening. As people walked by my bench I heard the whispers—"That's Kenny's daughter." "Poor thing." "She's so young."

Someone came close and I felt a brush of fabric against my leg as she sat down. I tightened my hands around my knees and listened quietly, not daring to look up. Her arm brushed my back.

"Leave her alone," another woman's voice said. "She doesn't want anyone near her." I didn't look up to see who it was, but my heart sank as those words rang over and over in my ears.

My parents had been divorced for a long time, my father an alcoholic before I was even born. My mom had fought hard to keep us together and sacrificed much so that my siblings and I would not have to see how terrible this disease of addiction was, but we all knew the truth anyway. I love my mother's meekness and compassion, which overflow from her sweet spirit. And her determination to fight for her children is something that I grew up with and that I now understand is deeply ingrained in me.

But my mother's desire to protect us and fight for us was perceived by some family members on my father's side as an attempt to keep us from our father, so for this reason she was not allowed to attend his funeral. Instead, she was forced to wait for us in the parking lot.

I spent the whole day sitting on that bench with my head between my knees trying hard to dream about other, happier days. And those three words kept ringing in my ears: *Leave her alone.*

As the tears dripped from my eyes, I wanted so bad to untangle myself and run outside to find my mom. *Be brave. Be brave. You are alone,* I told myself over and over. But I didn't have the courage to lift my head up out of my lap. I didn't want to see people staring at me. *I'm alone, and I have to be brave,* I told myself.

Suddenly I felt as if someone much bigger than me had picked me up and set me on his lap. For the first time that day, I raised my head from my knees to look around, but I was still on the bench. No one was there. No one had physically picked me up.

I looked right and left, confused. Who had made the bench shake? Who was there? But there was nobody. As I sagged down again and put my head back between my knees, these words flowed into my heart: *You are not alone. I am with you. You are not alone.*

A comforting feeling began to settle down over my hurting heart. I had no idea where these words were coming from or who said them. I only knew it was a different message from the one I had been telling myself.

Looking back, I realize that moment on the bench was the first time I ever interacted with the Lord, at least as far as I remember. He reached down and touched the heart of a small fatherless girl that day although I didn't really understand what it all meant.

Under normal circumstances I was the type of kid who would talk to everyone I saw, and if there was no one to talk to, I'd talk to my stuffed animals. My teachers usually considered my talkative nature more of a problem than a gift.

One day at school, on my way out to the playground, my class walked by a classroom where the kids were still inside with the door shut. I asked my teacher, "Why aren't these kids allowed to go to recess too?"

"Because they are different," she said carefully. "They go to recess at a special time." I didn't care if the kids were different. I liked different. So I decided to speak up and ask my teacher if I could stay in the classroom with the different kids. She smiled and agreed, and this is how I spent the rest of my recesses that year.

In high school I continued my busy and friendly ways, ignoring the taboos about who was "cool" and who was not. I signed up for many school clubs and kept every minute full with activities, and my busy schedule taught me organizational skills that would serve me well later. I was full of ideas and plans and projects, so I ended up becoming student council president and was even voted prom queen my senior year.

I loved surrounding myself with people and couldn't wait to go to college. My heart was set on Tulane University in New Orleans, but my mom couldn't afford the expensive tuition. I threw my energy into finding a scholarship, but every search came to a dead end. I determined the only way I could afford to go to Tulane was if I received the coveted Legislative Scholarship, a special full-ride scholarship that could be awarded only by someone who served in the Louisiana legislature.

In February of my senior year of high school, a special election was coming up in Lafayette, and I organized a voter drive at my school, signing up hundreds of new voters. Afterward I made an appointment with the winning congressional candidate, Joel Robideaux, and shared with him my dream of going to Tulane University. Often these congressional scholarship awards are political in nature, handed out as favors, but this time Mr. Joel understood my desire and rewarded my boldness in applying for the scholarship. He showed me that dreams do come true. My family and I had nothing to give him, but Mr. Joel gave me an amazing gift by sending me to Tulane for four years, all tuition and fees paid.

Freshman year went well, and I was busy as ever. But while I was preparing to return for my second year at Tulane, Hurricane Katrina roared through New Orleans. As the chaos of the storm and its aftermath settled in, we were told Tulane would not be open for classes in the fall. I had to find another school on the approved list that was provided for us. Overnight, I decided on Washington and Lee University in Lexington, Virginia. I would be there for at least a semester while hurricane repairs were carried out at Tulane.

That fall I was dropped off in the middle of an unfamiliar college campus. At least when I was at Tulane, I had high school friends attending and was very familiar with New Orleans. But here at Washington and Lee, it felt like my freshman year all over again, except this time I was in a faraway city at a university that I had never visited. I didn't know anyone and cried the whole way to my dorm room, dragging two suitcases of belongings behind me. I felt lost and completely alone, just as I did on the bench at that funeral home when I was seven. Alone in my dorm room I began to feel that I had made a huge mistake. *What am I doing here? I'm not sure I can do this. I don't know if I can be brave.*

But that familiar voice spoke to my spirit again, telling me I was not alone. I left my room to take a walk around the campus. Within minutes I met the friendliest guy, named Drew. Drew smiled, bounced around, and invited me to his church. I laughed as I declined his invitation. "I grew up Catholic," I said. "I've been to mass before. I already know what church is all about."

I threw myself into my schoolwork and tried to keep busy, but I kept remembering Drew's invitation. At the same time I felt a growing emptiness in my spirit. Over the next few weeks Drew kept inviting me to the small nondenominational church on campus, and I finally agreed. When I walked into the packed church, I heard the voice again, the One who had comforted me when I was just seven years old and feeling all alone.

Drew invited me to Bible studies and worship services. For the first time ever I began to understand what having a relationship with God was really all about. I began reading the Bible and realized I could pray all the time. God was always listening.

I returned to Tulane the next semester as planned, but I was different. My life had begun to change. Even though I couldn't exactly put my finger on what had changed, I felt different. I felt sure there was something, or Someone, guiding me.

On my way to cheerleading practice one night, waiting for a squad mate, I meandered down a hall and stumbled upon a Bible study taking place in a dorm lounge. After I had spent a few minutes peering in, someone invited me inside, and I sat down, intrigued by what they were talking about. Wide-eyed and completely enthralled, I missed the entire cheerleading practice that night. I started to attend the weekly Bible study.

Through this group my eyes were opened to the poverty in my own city. I joined an outreach group that handed out sandwiches on Saturdays to the thousands of homeless people living under bridges and in tents in downtown New Orleans, and my perspective of the poor began to change. The hurricane's devastation was unlike anything I had ever seen, and my heart was drawn to New Orleans's homeless. I learned more about the gospel, about freedom in Christ, and about the truth of His Word. My outlook on life began to shift dramatically. Jesus had broken through to my confused and closed heart.

I finished college and immediately entered the workforce, unsure of what God had planned for me. As I began my first job doing marketing for an industrial construction company, my eight-to-five position began to grow more monotonous and pointless. After months of inner struggle I wondered why I would ever need to know about rebar sizes and foundations on buildings. So I quit my marketing construction job and began working at Prevent Child Abuse Louisiana. Jesus continued stirring a desire for justice in my heart, but His preparation was much more intricate than I could ever imagine. My days at PCAL revolved around learning the importance of prevention and education for families and children. When my time at this job came to an end, I began working at Our Lady of the Lake Hospital, thinking I had finally found the place where God wanted me to serve.

But it wasn't until my visit to Bellevue Mountain in Haiti, where I saw the tamarind tree, that a place grabbed my heart so firmly and wouldn't let go. When my dreams about the tree wouldn't stop, I knew God was relentlessly pursuing me.

God was whispering, sometimes shouting, and I couldn't help but listen. After months of struggling I finally made the decision to return to Haiti . . . to stay.

And I can tell you right now, there is no way I would have moved to a place where it's so hot I literally sweat in the shower—where tarantulas, frogs, gigantic roaches, and other disgusting insects are your roommates; where I couldn't just hop in my car and zoom over to Chick-fil-A or Starbucks or even a grocery store—without the strength of my huge, all-powerful God. Only God could make me take this leap out of my comfortable life.

Through tears and trembling I quit my job, gave up my car, and had a garage sale to get rid of everything I couldn't pack in a couple of suitcases. It seemed like God's perfect timing since my roommate was getting married and moving to Australia the next month, but it was still exceptionally challenging. On the day of the sale, as I watched people digging through my apartment, my anxiety level grew. Every time someone picked up a cute pair of heels and complained the price was too high, I wanted to shout, "I paid sixty-five dollars for those, so that's a dang good deal!" But I didn't. I was determined to keep my composure. That unbearable weekend finally ended, and it was time to leave Louisiana.

I'd loved my job and my car and my life and my friends, and I felt torn. People close to me brought up concerns about my safety, about my plans that seemed to defy logic and reason, and about my money, which was limited. But I couldn't ever seem to shrug off that nudge from God, rooted on Bellevue Mountain. There were times I thought back to the people and children I'd met in Haiti, and my heart felt like a throbbing wound. I just could not ignore it anymore. I knew this desire to go was from the Lord, even if others didn't, so I gave in. *Okay, God. It's a green light until it's a red light.*

My mom drove me to the airport, with tears filling her eyes, as she hugged and kissed me good-bye, anxious about her baby traveling to a foreign land on an unknown, God-driven quest. Then I went through security and boarded the plane. Once again I was by myself. Except I knew for sure I wasn't really alone. As I found my seat, I knew the Lord was with me; He was in control. And I didn't need to hide my face anymore—I could lift my head with confidence, knowing my heavenly Father was always there.

I buckled my seat belt, took a deep breath, and closed my eyes. I was on my way.

FOUR

Rice, Beans, and Salami

Being unwanted, unloved, uncared for,
forgotten by everybody, I think that is a much
greater hunger, a much greater poverty
than the person who has nothing to eat.
—Mother Teresa

I couldn't shake the memory of Michaëlle throwing rocks at the blackbird. It was like a movie playing in my head. What would have happened if she'd hit one hard enough to kill it? Would she have pulled the feathers off and actually tried to start a small fire to cook it? I shuddered at the image my brain conjured up.

Of course I knew what it meant to be hungry after a workout or when I'd skipped a meal, but I didn't understand that kind of hunger. Why wasn't Michaëlle eating? The woman she lived with, who called herself Michaëlle's "aunt" even though she was not, looked as though she'd been getting enough to eat. Why not this little girl? She was growing and active and needed food. It made no sense.

I started looking at the children around my neighborhood

and wondering if they were getting enough to eat. I had heard on one of my previous trips that 50 percent of the population of Haiti is under sixteen years old. Fifty percent! This means half of the people in Haiti are children. I love the scripture where Jesus said, "Let the little children come to me, and do not hinder them, for the kingdom of heaven belongs to such as these" (Matt. 19:14). After registering Michaëlle for school, my next hope was to be able to feed her and the others around Bellevue Mountain.

I decided Saturday, just two days away, would be the day. I was going to feed as many children as I could up on the mountain. The problem was, I was still pretty much living off energy bars, and I didn't know how to cook Haitian food. I was sure the local children would not enjoy American-style food, such as spaghetti and meatballs or mac and cheese, so with the help of David and Bernard, I asked Say Say if she would be willing to cook some food for me.

I'd been watching how she carefully prepared the rice and beans she purchased each day in the market and cooked them in the front yard on the charcoal stove made of metal. Food and charcoal are expensive, so Say Say used only the amount she needed for her family, and there was never anything left over. I watched how careful she was to create a small, hot fire with her charcoal in the wire basket that held the cooking pot. In the mornings I also noticed the gray ashes coating the bottom of the stove and realized it was the same color as the road in front of the house. There are so many charcoal fires in Haiti that the smoke and the ash cover everything.

"Can Say Say cook for a hundred people?" I asked Bernard. After he spoke with her, she agreed, but said I needed to go to the market to buy rice, beans, coconut, charcoal, and more. She also suggested salami because "kids love it."

Knowing that I would never be able to find everything we needed, and since Bernard didn't frequent the Gressier market much, I asked Say Say to come with me. Off to the market we went, with Bernard tagging behind. I followed Say Say closely as she bustled quickly to the entrance of the outdoor market and began weaving in and out of the tiny but intimidating rows dotted with piles of onions, tomatoes, peppers, and more. The odor was strong, alternating between the smells of fresh produce and sewage. As I looked about the crowded market, I began to wonder if there were more people than produce.

After handing some money to Say Say, I quickly grabbed my journal to write down how much everything cost. Rummaging around my purse, I pulled out a pink highlighter and began jotting down amounts and costs. We continued to wind through the rows until I noticed the ground change from muddy brown to a deep black. I'd been watching my feet the whole time so I wouldn't trip or step on any produce, and now I was surprised to look up and see bags and bags of charcoal on blackened earth. People hunched around small buckets of charcoal pieces, their skin matching their merchandise.

As we finished with a purchase of charcoal, we called a *tap-tap* to help transport everything we bought back to my house. The brightly colored truck pulled to a stop in front of us, and we climbed on, struggling to fit the enormous bag of charcoal, rice, beans, salami, filtered water (packaged in little, individual plastic bags), and other ingredients among the tight crowd on board. The tap-tap lurched forward, and we headed out of the market. Once my house came into view, we tapped the side of the truck loudly, and it lurched to a stop. Once again we fought the crowd on board to get all our things off. We stood in our front yard, where Say Say planned to cook, and I took a deep breath and smiled at my new friends. The adventure was successful, and word began to get out about my Saturday project. A few people in the community even volunteered to help Say Say cook the food. What a blessing!

I awoke very early that Saturday morning, just before daybreak, to see the team had begun cooking. I was anxious, wondering what it was going to be like having a bunch of children in a big open space up on Bellevue Mountain. But the biggest concern that was repeating in my mind was, *Will I have enough food for them?* Since the cooking was well underway with plenty of hands to help, I simply watched the meticulous preparation. After a while I realized I wasn't needed at the house. I felt restless, so I decided to go ahead and walk to the top of the mountain to pray under the tamarind tree and wait for the tap-tap to arrive with the food. It was scheduled to be on Bellevue Mountain around four in the afternoon.

Within minutes of my arrival, even though there were hours before the food would arrive, children started coming up to Bellevue Mountain from every direction. Some were extremely young. *How do they even know where the feeding is supposed to be?* Other kids were sweating profusely, and I wondered how far they had walked. As each child arrived, I smiled and said, *"Bonswa!"* and waved for them to come play with the others.

Hours later, at around 4:30 p.m., Bernard arrived, an example of what I'd come to learn—that things in Haiti never happen on time or the way they are supposed to. Bernard, who was working as my translator, is a smart, passionate, young guy who loves kids and the Lord. He had grown up in a rough neighborhood in Haiti. The few Brooklyn deportees who had taught him English were now living in his same neighborhood.

We started out with a prayer led by Bernard, and then we sang a popular school song, *"C'est la Journee"* ("This Is the Day"). I recognized the tune and was able to sing along in English. As I looked at each child's face, I was overjoyed. *Everyone is a child of God. Everyone has been born with a beautiful purpose from Christ.* Did they know? I wanted them to understand this, to really know and believe they were beautiful and worthy and special. As we sang, they began to smile and laugh and dance. Glancing around, I saw children with tinted orange hair, from malnutrition; tiny feet, barefoot and dirty; yet on every face was a beautiful white-teethed grin. The mountaintop was transformed into a lively playground by their sudden joy.

While we were singing and playing, the tap-tap arrived, nearly an hour late. The driver parked down the field from us, and one of the local pastors, his wife, and some of their church members helped the children line up to eat. Michaëlle's aunt volunteered to help serve, so we climbed into the back of the tap-tap and began scooping food onto the plates. Each child received a big plate of rice and beans with salami on top. It sounded gross to me, but they loved it.

We served dozens of children. After a half hour or so, I realized that the line continued to stretch around the back of the truck so I couldn't see how many children were still waiting in line. I was worried about running out of food for them. These children were truly hungry, had walked long distances, and had stood patiently in line for a plate. *All right, Lord,* I prayed. *This is going to be like the fish and loaves, right?*

I was freaking out a bit, but as we came to the end of the food and began scraping the pots, the line seemed to come to an end too. I looked up and saw just one little girl remaining, and my heart leapt—we had just enough food for her. I reached down to scoop up the last bit of rice but just then looked up and saw a young boy approach. "I didn't get any," he said, embarrassed, his sunken-in eyes looking at the ground. *Oh, no!* My heart sank.

I handed the full plate to a man who was helping so he could give it to the little girl, but he misunderstood and handed it instead to the boy who had just walked up. I tried to tell the man to give the food to the girl who had been waiting, but it was too late. I looked down into the pot again and moved my large serving spoon. There was exactly enough rice and beans for this young girl. I couldn't believe it. I was sure we had run out of rice and beans on the last plate. Immediately I was reminded that I am not the one planning this; God is. He has every grain of rice counted for these children.

Afterward we ran and played and sang and danced again. I had so many children trying to hold my hand; it made me wish there were a hundred of me, just to show each child how special each of them truly is. The most beautiful thing about the whole day was how many children came up to me, looked me in the eye, said, *"Mesi,"* and then kissed my cheek. Bernard said for most of them, it was their first, and probably only, meal of the day.

As I walked back down the mountain, spent but happy, I started to get a little picture of the work ahead of me in Haiti. *So this is what life is about. This is what being the hands and feet of Jesus means. I can't change the fact that it's perfectly normal for young children to walk up and down a slippery, steep path with a bucket of water on their heads. I can't change the fact that people here are in survival mode and sometimes all these children eat is rice and beans once a day, if that. I can't change the political situation or force people to care for other people.*

I crossed through the mango grove, a new determination in my step. *Now I know what I can do. I can show these children love. I can show them joy. I can show them compassion. I can show each of these children Jesus. Force will not affect Haiti. Politics will not have an impact on Haiti. Jesus will.*

When I arrived back at my crooked gate, I looked at my house in a whole new way. I'd been feeling a little sorry for myself with the chilly bucket showers and the light switches that didn't work. *But every one of my neighbors lives in a tent or half-open house. No one has running water here. No one has electricity. I don't have electricity or running water, but I have a roof and four walls, so I am still better off than most of Gressier.*

As I opened the gate and went inside, I suddenly felt exhausted. I took a quick bath, crawled inside my mosquito net, and lay in the darkness, thanking God for what He had done that day. Just before I dropped off to sleep, I thought of Michaëlle. She had been on the mountain with all the other children, and her little stomach was full tonight. That made me smile. No throwing rocks at birds for her today.

I thought of her sweet brown eyes and how she'd fiercely hugged Bernard and me with her thin brown arms. *Lord, please watch over Michaëlle and keep her safe. Let her feel loved and cared for and precious, because she is.*

I drifted off to sleep. And that night the voodoo drums were silent.

FIVE

A *Restavek*

A person's a person, no matter how small.
—Dr. Seuss

*N*on," she shouted, clinging with all of her strength to the branches of a scrawny little bush in the mango grove. Michaëlle was refusing to let go. It was a Sunday morning, and we were halfway up the path to the blue tent on the mountain where she lived. With tears streaming down her face, yelling and screaming hysterically, words poured out of her so fast I couldn't understand even one syllable. I crept closer and sat down next to her in the dirt. When I got down on her level, I realized I didn't have to understand any Haitian Creole to know what was going on. I didn't need to understand a single word to see that her face was filled with fear, fear of returning to her tent. I was rocked by the waves of terror emanating from her tiny seven-year-old body.

My heart ached, and I felt anxiety rising inside because I knew I couldn't really talk to her, even though I tried. In my most soothing and confident voice, I called her Micha (pronounced "Mee-ka," my new nickname for her) and told her everything was going to be okay, but it didn't seem to help. After a few minutes of feeling completely helpless I, too, burst into tears as I stared, transfixed, at her frail body shaking and plastered to the dusty bush. I'd never before felt so helpless, and I begged God to show me what to do. *Why is this happening? Please! Tell me what to do, and I'll do it.*

The waves of fear and anxiety rolled over me, and I almost felt as though I was drowning. I felt alone, confused, and frustrated. Words weren't working, so I began to sing, in a quiet and thin voice, as the words to "When I Am Afraid" came out of my mouth. Over and over I sang this song, based on one of David's psalms, for Micha and for myself. Each time I sang it I felt a little spark of comfort, and I prayed Micha did too. I finally managed to pry her off of the bush and sit her in my lap, her tiny body still shaking. As we sat there together, with me still quietly singing, I could feel her body begin to relax and her breathing slow down. I prayed over her and held her tight. All I could do was repeat in English that I loved her.

She leaned back for a few minutes; then I felt her body tense up. I watched as her back grew stiff and her stoic face returned, almost like her shell was hardening again. She pushed my arms away, stood up, and walked up the path. As I called after her, "Micha!" she began to run ahead full speed without turning around. I watched her disappear up the hill, a small puff of gray dust hanging in the air where she'd started to run.

Should I follow her? I wondered. But I was exhausted by her random outburst and my attempts to comfort her, so I turned around and walked back to my house. With each step I asked myself if I was helping her or hurting her by bringing her to my house each Saturday evening after the feeding to spend the night, take a bath, and have her hair braided.

Micha's aunt and the others in the tent where she lived didn't seem to love her. At least they didn't show it when I was around. It was so confusing. *Why is Micha so sad all the time? Why is she the one that seems to be doing all of the household chores and all the work? Why doesn't she want to go back home?* The questions and curiosity and confusion swirled around in my brain and wouldn't stop. My stomach clenched, telling me there was something deeper happening and I needed to find out what it was. After the emotionally exhausting morning I wrenched open the front gate, crossed the front yard, and burst through the front door, frantic to find my cell phone. I needed answers, and I didn't care how expensive the Internet data charges were going to be.

I turned on my cell phone and pulled up Google. Then I typed in the three words that would forever change my life: *Haiti + child + servant.*

A word I'd never heard before popped up in big, black, bold letters: *restavek.*

I froze, staring at the word on my cell phone screen for a good five minutes before scrolling down. *There is actually a name for this way of treating children in Haiti.* My mind reeled in confusion. I didn't want to believe it, but as I continued reading, my head felt as though it would explode with this horrific discovery. The word *restavek* (sometimes spelled with a *c* instead of a *k)* is translated "to stay with" and is a common arrangement in Haiti, where parents force a child to live with another family because they are very poor or because of parental death or illness. Sometimes it includes the child being sold, kidnapped, or borrowed for a period of time.

I read a statement by the United Nations, condemning the restavek system as a "modern form of slavery" where even young children are put to work as laborers and treated as less than human.[1] The majority of these restaveks are girls between the ages of four and fifteen, and they are responsible for all of the cooking, cleaning, laundry, and fetching of water for their households. Additionally, restaveks often suffer severe abuse and are very rarely enrolled in school.

There was much more, but I'd seen enough, and I put down my phone. The room felt as though it was spinning. "Micha," I gasped. Like an overwhelming rush, everything started to make sense. This is why she wasn't in school when I met her. This is why I always saw her carrying heavy buckets of water or washing clothes in a tub outside the tent or surrounded by endless piles of dirty dishes. *This is why she sleeps under a table on cardboard.*

I remembered the day we came to enroll her in school; her aunt brought some chairs outside of the tent for us, and she wouldn't sit down even when I patted the chair next to me. She'd whispered something in my ear, and Bernard had translated: "Chairs are for adults. I can't sit."

Like a slideshow, images from the last few weeks popped up in my head as I remembered the many young girls I'd seen around Gressier who seemed to be working constantly. I had wondered why they stared down at the ground, eyes glassy and sad, and shoulders drooping. It was all starting to make sense, and I knew I had just made a life-changing discovery; I was finally able to put a finger on the disturbing feeling that had crawled its way up into my heart every time I passed these children. It was as if I could see the darkness of the situation and the evil behind it. I realized what the Holy Spirit had been stirring up in me the past few weeks, and I felt as though the Lord was igniting a fire inside me.

Children's faces, one after another, popped into my head as I realized that Bellevue Mountain and much of Gressier were full of restaveks in an epidemic of child slavery. It made me sick to my stomach that I had been walking around this community for the last few weeks, knowing that something was wrong, wanting to question the situation, but not knowing how to begin. And it made me even sicker to know that so many Haitians had accepted and participated in this form of slavery in their own country with their own people.

I couldn't find any firm statistics, but organizations that had studied the situation estimated that 300,000 to 500,000 children in Haiti are restaveks. I couldn't get my mind and heart around that number. I still can't. I never will.

Over the next few days I began to ask questions, read, research, and soak in every last bit of information on restaveks, no matter how disheartening or disturbing. I wanted to know everything there was to know about this crisis and what we could do to free these children in bondage.

One restavek named Jean-Robert Cadet grew up in Haiti but moved to America with his "aunt" when he was a teenager. He eventually left her, got an education, and wrote a book about his experiences. Here's how he described the system:

> Restavecs are treated worse than slaves, because they don't
> cost anything and their supply seems inexhaustible. They . . .
> are made to sleep on cardboard, either under the kitchen table
> or outside on the front porch. For any minor infraction they
> are severely whipped with the cowhide that is still being made
> exclusively for that very purpose. . . . My clothes were rags and
> neighborhood children shouted "restavec" whenever they saw

me in the streets. I always felt hurt and deeply embarrassed, because to me the word meant motherless and unwanted.[2]

I had seen dozens of restaveks since I'd moved to Haiti, and I didn't even recognize it. *I've been so naïve.*

On a walk with Bernard, I asked, "How do you know when a child is a restavek?"

"You just know," he said.

Three minutes later I saw a tiny girl by the side of the road. She looked frail, like she could break in half. She wore a woman's skirt, pulled up to serve as a dress, and she was barefoot, dirty, and carrying two heavy water jugs, filled to the brim. She stopped and waited as we passed, her dull, sullen eyes following us. Bernard took one glance at her and said, "See her there? She's one."

That hour in the mango grove with a traumatized Micha changed me, and I looked at the children of Gressier through eyes sharpened by my newfound knowledge. The Lord had begun to remove the scales from my eyes and I couldn't go back. I called my mom to tell her what I'd discovered about Micha, bawling into the phone and telling her I had to do something to help. And I knew cooking pots of beans and rice or singing songs with kids wasn't going to be enough.

SIX

The Orphanage

When you truly accept that those children in
some far off place in the global village have the
same value as you in God's eyes or even in just
your eyes, then your life is forever changed,
you see something that you can't un-see.
—Bono

The first time I walked through the red, six-foot gate into the courtyard of Son of God Orphanage, I felt in my spirit as if a dark cloud was blocking any sort of light from reaching inside. Immediately I was overwhelmed by the sheer number of children who quickly attached themselves to me, grabbing on and wanting to be held and touched. I slowly tried to make my way to a concrete bench, trying not to fall or trip over someone. As soon as I sat down, I couldn't even count the number of hands on me, rubbing my face, braiding my hair, patting my legs, and even touching my painted toenails in my flip-flops.

I had heard briefly about Son of God Orphanage and had the urge to visit for some unknown reason—maybe to see it with my own eyes or maybe because there was a tug on my heart that I couldn't quite put my finger on. The orphanage was in a three-story, gray, concrete-block building in a crowded city not far from Port-au-Prince. On the front of the building were open hallways lined with red metal railings, stacked on top of each other and overlooking a dusty gray courtyard.

Sitting on the concrete bench with dozens of children's hands pulling the hair on my arms, I only had an hour to spend at Son of God. Honestly, I was relieved when the time was up. Since this visit was on a trip before my decision to move to Gressier, I left thinking I would never return and remembering only lots of children, dark hallways, and bad smells.

Despite the heaviness of my first visit to the orphanage, one of the first things God prompted me to do after I moved to Haiti and settled in Gressier was to return and check on these children.

I had learned there were some organizations in the States that supported Son of God Orphanage, so when I returned in January 2011, I hoped it would be different, better, maybe infused with a little more joy and light. I took a deep breath, knocked on the gate, and felt dozens of eyes glaring down on me from different corners of the broken building. The gate creaked open, and I was met by a young girl who grabbed my arm and led me down a dark hallway, spouting something in Creole that meant nothing to me. She led me into a room on the ground floor of the building and showed me some chairs with a coffee table in between. The room was dark and windowless; there were piles of unmarked boxes stacked up in the corners with sheets thrown over them. The air felt sticky, and I was sweating profusely, so I propped myself on the end of a floral fabric-covered chair. I looked around and saw little eyes peeping at me from everywhere—behind, in front, and even out of the window. I heard a few giggles and some quiet scurrying.

I sat and waited. For some reason there was an indescribable pressure building in my core, and a few times I thought about just standing up and leaving. I got anxious and looked at my watch after what seemed like an eternity, but it had barely been three minutes. *Why am I here? Why am I waiting? Am I really supposed to be here?*

I was already starting to doubt the impulse that had brought me there. Maybe the tug on my heart had meant something else. Before I could finish my thought, a round, bald Haitian man walked slowly into the room. Although he greeted me with a big smile on his face, my heart jumped. I felt as if I had been physically shoved back in my chair even though he was still a good ten feet away.

The man approached me, murmured something, and stuck out his hand. I shook it, and he sat down across the coffee table from me. He started talking so fast in Creole he didn't seem to take a breath. I laughed nervously and said ineptly the only words I really knew in his language, besides hello and good-bye: *"No pale Kreyòl." I don't speak Creole.*

He laughed at that, his belly jiggling, and then looked to his right as if this was something that had been rehearsed a hundred times. Another hand stuck out in my direction, and I shook it. This time it was a boy in his late teens who could speak broken English. "This Pastor Joseph Roumain.* He is director for orphanage. He is called Pastor Joe."

I smiled and nodded and explained that I had visited before and now lived nearby in Gressier and wanted to visit more

---

* Name has been changed.

frequently to spend time with the children. As the boy translated my words, Pastor Joe seemed to listen, but his shoulders shrugged, and his face didn't show much emotion. I looked at him, waiting for any sort of cue and expecting a question or two. Instead, he snapped something at the boy, who turned his head to me and asked hesitantly, "Have you brought something?"

Was I supposed to bring gifts? Confused and a little embarrassed, I looked up at him and said I had not brought anything. Pastor Joe said something else in Creole, then abruptly stood up and walked out of the room. I watched him leave and heard the boy whisper to me quietly, "You can go visit the children."

I walked back down the narrow, gloomy hallway to the courtyard. The stench was so bad, worse than I remembered, that I almost turned around and left. Suddenly a small child caught my eye. Walking toward her, I tried to ignore the smell of feces, urine, and sweat in the air. I picked up the sweet, frail child and held her in my arms. I could feel her breathing slowly. I sat down and looked around at the other children near me. Their hollow eyes stared blankly at me, and their thin bodies seemed to contain no energy. On this visit there was no laughing, no giggles, no playing with my hair or inspecting my painted toenails.

I had so many questions to ask but no words; the language barrier was drowning me. I spotted an older girl and greeted her in English, hoping she might know at least a few words. "What is wrong with the children?" I asked, but she shook her head as if she had no idea what my words meant. I repeated the question to a boy next to her. Nothing. Then from behind me I heard someone mutter in English with a strong Haitian accent, "No food."

I turned around to see a rail-thin boy who looked to be in his teens. He looked at me with big, serious eyes and repeated himself, louder this time. "No food. Three days."

What? No food? These kids haven't eaten for three days?

I asked him again. "No food?"

"Three days," he said again, nodding his head.

My jaw dropped, and I was flooded with emotion. I was so shocked and couldn't believe this could happen in an orphanage with supposed American support, run by a pastor, and named "Son of God." Instantaneously my naïveté began to dissolve, and I was rocked by the sadness and lethargy of the children. After a few more minutes inside, I had to get out. I felt selfish, but I couldn't handle what I was seeing and what I had learned. I managed to make it outside the gate before the tears began to flow. *What do I do, Lord?*

I was upset and fuming and began muttering in outrage like a crazy person as I walked toward Bernard, who was waiting outside to take me back to Gressier. He didn't say anything, just patted my shoulder awkwardly in an attempt to comfort me. We headed back home in a tap-tap, and I didn't want to talk or make eye contact with anyone. I felt like a hermit crab, trying to scramble back deep into its shell, and Bernard and I rode back in complete silence. My raging emotions drowned out the shouts of "*blan*," *white*, by children on the street, and the piercing stares of the other passengers in the truck didn't even faze me. After the tap-tap let us off in Gressier, I tried to make sense of my feelings and confusion on the twenty-minute walk back to my house.

When I opened the front gate of my house, I was met with the amazing smell of our only meal of the day. My stomach was now used to granola bars in the morning along with one large afternoon meal. Say Say had just finished cooking rice and black bean sauce for dinner. I took one look at the food, thought of the starving children I had just left in the orphanage, and snapped back at Bernard, "You can eat it all or give it to the neighbors." Then I grabbed my Bible and my flashlight from my room and headed for the roof. The only thing I knew to do, besides cry, was scour the pages of the Bible for some sort of instruction.

When I thought of Pastor Joe, I felt again the intense emotions that had rushed over me at the orphanage. I kept thinking, *Maybe it's that I've only been here a couple of weeks, and I'm just really homesick. Maybe I don't understand the culture here, or how orphanages work.* But no matter what excuse I came up with, I couldn't label the emotions plaguing me when I thought of the pastor.

One thing was clear—I needed to go back and visit the orphanage again soon, so I began asking God for guidance, clarity, and courage. My flesh wanted to forget what I had seen and to stay put in Gressier. But over the next few days God continued to burden my heart with such unexplainable force that I returned to the orphanage in less than a week.

This time the gate opened before I could knock, and a young boy gave me a little grin and pulled me gently inside. I asked for Pastor Joe, but the boy shook his head. *Is the pastor not here?* I let out a breath of relief when I realized he was out, but I still felt heaviness in my chest as I walked into the dark corridor.

I headed toward the back courtyard because that was normally where the children gathered. On my way down the hallway, I stopped when I saw a little girl who looked about two years old sitting alone on the ground. Her top lip was swollen and oozing yellow. I threw my hands in the air and asked the kids gathered around me what was wrong with her. Silence. *This place cannot get any worse,* I thought.

The next second, it did. One of the teenagers picked up the little girl, turned her around, and flung the skirt of her soiled blue dress up before I could even blink. I gasped at the worst burn I have ever seen. It looked as though someone had taken a bite out of the back of her thigh. It was obvious by the yellow color and the stench that it had been there awhile.

Although I have a sister who is a veterinarian and a brother who is a paramedic, I have always closed my eyes at blood, burns, or surgeries on TV. I looked around wide-eyed and panicked, yelling for someone to help. Realizing there was no one other than a bunch of little children, I stopped yelling and grabbed one of the older boys who knew some English. "Soap? Water?" I asked slowly.

He nodded, without blinking, and tugged on my arm. I carefully picked up the little girl and followed the boy back down the dark hallway to a small room. The boy stopped in front of a closed door with a sign: "Dr. Roumain." *Okay, so he's a pastor and a doctor. He must not know about this wound because he would have known how to treat her.*

I looked back at the boy. "How long has she been like this?"

He squinted his eyes, and I could tell he didn't understand. I tried again, pointing at the wound, saying, "How long?" He hesitated, then mumbled, "Twelve?"

I put her on her stomach, found some rubber gloves for my hands, and began to gently dab at the wound with soap, water, and gauze. To my shock, the little girl whimpered a few times, then was quiet. As I cleaned her burn, my tears mixed into the soapy water, and I began singing. As I picked maggots from the wound, I sang louder and louder. A few times I could feel acid crawling up my throat, and I felt that I might vomit, but then I remembered the slew of children staring at me from the doorway. I thought about shutting the door to keep them out, but there was no electricity in the room, and I needed the light. Turning back around, I sang louder over her poor, burned thigh.

Just as I was almost finished cleaning her wound, Pastor Joe walked in. He looked at me and smiled arrogantly. If I had known Creole, he might have gotten punched in the face with some angry words. But I didn't, so I did the next best thing—I handed him the wad of blood-and-pus–covered gauze. He shook his head firmly, refused to take it, and waved his hand back at me to continue.

I looked at the little boy, raised my eyebrows, and asked, "Doctor?" The little boy took one look up at Pastor Joe, turned, and ran away. I handed the gauze to Pastor Joe again, hoping he would take it. He shook his head again.

Hot tears burned my cheeks as I raised my voice and, not caring if he understood my English, I shouted, "I have never even watched a medical show. If you are a doctor, then you know what to do. So do it!" I swung around to face him one last time and again held the damp gauze out in front of me. He grabbed the box of gloves next to me, put on a pair, then reached over and snatched the gauze out of my hand to finish.

I watched Pastor Joe sprinkle some antibiotic powder on the wound, and I made a vow, just a few weeks into my Haitian journey, that I would learn wound care and I would not be afraid. *It can't get much worse.*

As Pastor (Doctor?) Joe finished cleaning the wound, he turned the sweet girl over and held her away from him as if she were diseased. I took her back. Just as quickly as he arrived, he left, stomping away and mumbling something about the *"blan."*

I gave the girl to one of the older children who was looking on, then sat in a chair, bent over, wanting so bad to lose it, to scream and sob and shake my fist at the heavens. But there were dozens of children looking on with fear in their eyes, so instead, I sucked it all in. I held my breath, turned around, forced a half smile, and waved good-bye as I walked out. It was all I could stand for one day, but I knew I would be back.

SEVEN

Respire: Breathe

I have found that there are three stages in
every great work of God: first, it is impossible,
then it is difficult, then it is done.
—Hudson Taylor

H ere, you can use this table to set up your stuff," said the young woman before she walked away.

My mom and I looked at each other. *Stuff? What stuff?*

I looked over at the adjacent tables covered with artfully arranged logo tablecloths, photo displays, and business cards. I looked back at our table with absolutely nothing on it except maybe a light coating of dust.

"It's okay, Meg," my mom said in her soothing and encouraging voice.

After living in Haiti by myself for almost two months, I needed to get back to the States to take care of some organizational business. I had established an official nonprofit so that I could raise funds to pay for the work I was doing. I'd tried hard to brainstorm ideas for the name, and I'd kept thinking of how easily I could breathe in Gressier compared to the concrete-covered polluted city of Port-au-Prince. God brought to mind the scripture in Job that exclaims, "The Spirit of God has made me; the *breath* of the Almighty gives me life" (33:4, emphasis mine). I Googled the word *breathe* in Creole, and *respire* (ress-purr-ay) came up. Not knowing exactly what our mission would be, I'd briefly written that Respire Haiti was created "to help children in Haiti."

Before I left Gressier for the trip to Louisiana, I received an e-mail from Bret Pinson, a man who had been instrumental in helping me get the job at Our Lady of the Lake Hospital—the job I'd quit when I moved to Haiti. I hesitated to respond at first, mostly because I wondered if he was going to ask why I quit such a great job. I had streams of negative thoughts flowing through my mind but decided to e-mail him back anyway. He responded with a brief, "Call me when you are stateside so we can meet."

When I landed in Louisiana, I had only two weeks and knew I needed to make every day productive. I didn't have a clear picture of what that meant yet, but I did call Mr. Pinson, and we set a time to meet.

That same afternoon, Dennis Eenigenburg, a friendly Louisiana pastor, joined us along with his wife. I told them my story, and after a thirty-minute conversation, Pastor Dennis asked if I'd be willing to give a ten-minute talk to his congregation. Seeing my anxiety level rise with the thought of speaking in front of a church, he quickly added that there would be two other nonprofits participating, so it would be low-key.

"Yes, I would love to do it," my mouth said, while my brain was saying, *No! What in the world am I going to talk about for ten whole minutes?*

I showed up at his church the following Sunday, my only

visual aid a jump drive containing a few pictures taken with my cell phone. After seeing the displays the other nonprofits set up, I felt very unprepared. As worship finished and Pastor Dennis invited the first organization up front, I watched nervously as a very well-composed man walked forward and began explaining his incredible project working with underprivileged children in Baton Rouge, Louisiana. My heart started beating so hard I could hear it vibrating in my ears.

The rest of what he said was a blur until I heard Pastor Dennis say, "And our next speaker is . . ." I let out my breath in a whoosh of relief when he didn't call my name, but I still wanted to run out of the room. I watched a well-put-together video about the second group's mission, and before I knew it, they were finishing up. And that left . . . me.

My heart was beating like crazy again, and my palms started sweating. My mind jumped around with everything I wanted to say. Then he called my name. "Please welcome Megan Boudreaux of Respire Haiti." Numb, I stood up and took a few hesitant steps down the aisle. Pastor Dennis, whom I'd known for only three days, said a few words about what I was doing in Gressier. When I got up to the front, I swallowed hard, not entirely sure words would come out of my mouth. Pastor Dennis handed me the microphone and I said, "Hello. My name is Megan," in a shaky voice. But no one seemed to be listening. Instead, their eyes looked beyond me, and I turned around to see what everyone was staring at.

I almost dropped the microphone as I saw Michaëlle's picture, six feet tall, on the screen behind me. It was the picture from the mountain, in the ragged yellow tank top she wore as a dress, hanging off one shoulder. I turned back around, looked at the faces, and breathed out. This time when I began speaking, the words flowed easily out of me. I shared the story of Michaëlle and her battle for food, a safe place to sleep, education, and love. I explained what a restavek is and how Michaëlle was not actually free, even at seven years old. I saw jaws drop at the mention of child slavery. Then I clicked to the next picture, with hundreds of children eating at the Saturday feeding program. I looked out and saw shock and anger turn to empathy and hope.

Then I spoke about this incredible place called Bellevue Mountain. And with that it was over. Everyone clapped, and I smiled, feeling the sweating and rapid heartbeat begin again. I beelined it, head down, back to my seat next to my mom. As I snuggled next to her arm, wanting to hide from everyone looking at me, she held my hand and whispered, "You did well."

After the service ended, Pastor Dennis made an announcement about the tables. "These folks will be at their tables to answer any questions you might have," he said. I thought about our empty table, looked at my mom again, and almost laughed as we both raised our eyebrows and rolled our eyes just a tiny bit. Then we got up and headed back to the lobby to stand behind our table.

I felt awkward, but people immediately began coming up to us. As the first person walked up, he held a check out to me. I almost didn't understand what he wanted me to do. *Money?* I almost said it out loud. *You want to give us money? We're a 501(c)(3), but we don't even have a bank account yet!*

I thanked him and took the check without looking at the amount. I gave it to my mom. Then it happened again, and again and again. People came with checks, cash, questions, and prayers. Mom started stacking the donations in a pile on the back corner of the table. I sensed the Spirit of God so strongly, and I kept looking over at my mom, who had been hesitant, as any mother would have been, to let her twenty-four-year-old daughter move to a foreign country alone.

We repeated the same schedule for a second service, and back at the table there were more checks, more cash, more people encouraging us and wanting to know more. When it was all over, Mr. Pinson came up, and with a huge smile and no hesitation, he asked, "How much money did you raise?"

I looked at him, confused. My mom and I were so overwhelmed with the questions and expressions of support that we hadn't even thought to count the money. We moved over to a corner and began to look at the checks made out to Respire Haiti: $500, $150, $250, $50, $1,000. On and on it went. Tears began flowing down my mom's face, and Mr. Pinson looked so happy and excited for us. Then we were done and wrote the total on a piece of paper: $39,525.

I had no words. I looked over at my mom. Her eyes were squeezed shut as if to say, *I get it, Lord. I understand.*

An additional $10,000 came in by the end of the day, bringing our total to nearly $50,000. That night my mom slept with all the cash and checks at the foot of her bed. The next day we opened a bank account, still in disbelief at how God had worked this out. It far surpassed what Pastor Dennis or Mr. Pinson thought would happen.

When we made the deposit, I looked at Mom and said, "I guess I won't have to keep using my savings to pay for the feeding program and the children's school fees." The whole experience was surreal. As I headed back to Haiti after my two weeks were up, I thought about how I'd been going home to Louisiana to plan how to raise funds, to plan how I might be able to get support. Little did I know this was the beginning of the Holy Spirit working through me on Bellevue Mountain. I was learning to close my eyes, open my hands, and let Him lead me.

During my trip to Louisiana, I had a hard time being present mentally. I kept thinking about the small group of kids in Gressier who had been meeting for school lessons in a dilapidated church with an even more dilapidated chalkboard. There were no benches, no books, and only a few teachers who struggled to be heard over the noise of the busy national highway, just yards away. The students had no schedule and seemed to come and go as they pleased. They also did not have uniforms—*the* sign that a Haitian school is legitimate.

I'd been bringing more and more children to the church for school, and I'd begun to realize that to be a real school we needed more teachers, more supplies, and more space. My heart was full at what God had done, and I was excited about the work still ahead.

On my first morning back in Haiti, I woke up early to the crowing of the neighborhood roosters, a sound I had not missed in the States. I splashed some freezing cold water on my face from the bucket I'd used to take a shower the night before and grabbed a granola bar on the way out the door. I crossed the dirt road and headed to the familiar path up to Bellevue Mountain.

The sun was hot on the back of my neck. I'd forgotten to put on sunscreen, so I quickened my pace and smiled as I climbed up the mountain, anxious to see everyone and everything I'd missed while I was gone. There was always so much activity all around the tamarind tree. I usually saw a mix of cows, horses, and goats along with the precious Haitian people, smiling children, and

Micha, of course, although in the mornings she was usually busy fetching water or doing other chores around the tent.

But this morning, when I arrived at the flat top of the mountain, no one was there. I walked toward the tree and heard a squeaky voice cry out. I turned around, and there she was, smiling big with her toothless grin. "Micha!" I smiled back and hugged her as she ran into my arms.

Micha opened her mouth and I knew what was going to come out—crazy-fast Haitian Creole that confused me more than ever. Instead, I heard her clearly say, "I missed you. Where did you go?"

What? My eyes widened, and I tilted my head, trying to see if I'd heard her correctly or if it was just my imagination. Out of her mouth came, *"Mwen te sonje ou! Kote ou te ale?"* but somehow I had understood her words.

She must have thought I didn't hear her, because I didn't respond, so she said it again louder. "I missed you! Where did you go?"

My stomach churned as I listened to her sweet voice. Micha was speaking Haitian Creole; it was the only language she knew. But I had understood her as if she were speaking English. I opened my mouth and answered back. As the words came out, my eyes widened even more, and tears started spilling down my cheeks.

Micha smiled big as she heard me say in Creole how much I missed her too. She hugged me again, and as I hugged her back, I felt an explosion of excitement and energy deep in my spirit. It was as if the frustration, disappointment, and timidity of those first two months in Haiti had been launched out of my being. I felt a rush of energy, and I turned around and sprinted down the path.

I wasn't exactly sure what was going on or where I was going. Up ahead I saw Pastor and Madame Charles sitting in broken chairs in front of their church. They smiled big and waved, welcoming me home. I had met Pastor and his wife a few weeks earlier in Gressier and occasionally attended their church. As I approached them, I addressed them in Creole. They both stood up and smiled, looking a little confused. Pastor jokingly said, "Did you go home and study Creole for two weeks?"

He could see the shock and surprise on my face as I understood him and shook my head no. Pastor and Madame Charles looked at me, then looked at each other, and without a trace of disbelief they both shot out of their chairs and walked back and forth, waving their hands in the air, praising God. *"Glwa pou Bondye!"* they exclaimed, again and again. "Thank You, Jesus!"

My mind could not grasp what was happening. I opened my mouth again to speak, and the smoothest Creole poured out. After months of struggling, even to ask a child her name, and being incredibly timid to speak, this was happening.

I called Bernard, asking him to come quickly to Gressier. When he arrived, I explained what had happened to me, and he broke out in a huge grin. This gift was unsettling to me, so his smile was such a comfort.

"I don't need to translate for you anymore." He laughed. And I laughed with him, starting to understand what God had done.

The gift of speaking, reading, and writing Haitian Creole is something I had prayed for almost in passing. Trying to work alone in Gressier was so frustrating, and not being able to speak to the very children God had called me to help was also very challenging.

"You should speak Creole," was a comment I heard often. "Aren't you from Louisiana? Don't they speak French there? You should know this. This should be easy for you." But I couldn't. And I'd regretted, daily, that I hadn't paid more attention to French in high school. I regretted even more that in college I'd chosen to study Spanish because now it was no help at all.

Haitian Creole is the native language spoken by everyone who grows up in Haiti. It's a blend of eighteenth-century French and Portuguese, Spanish, Taino (a language from the original, indigenous people of Haiti), and West African languages. Haitian Creole has its own spelling, pronunciation, and accent. The wealthy upper class, a small percentage of the population, also speak French. Business and legal matters in the country are typically conducted in French, but most Haitians don't get far enough in school to learn to speak French fluently, much less to read or write it.

Speaking Creole was going to help me connect with the people of Gressier. As my heartbeat and breathing finally began to slow, I felt the Lord's comforting hand. He was directing this. He was in control, and He was making a way. I turned around to face the church. This one-room building was filling up with students—sixty sweaty, loud, rowdy children, and we needed more space. When I'd started Respire Haiti, I knew I wanted to work with children but honestly had no clue what form that would take. Even though I had been in Gressier for just a little more than two months, God was now making it very clear that He wanted Respire Haiti to focus on education.

And the more He revealed to me the problems in Gressier, the clearer the vision grew to include not only encouraging and empowering children but also, most importantly, fighting for the freedom of restaveks.

Fear of the future still plagued me, and I had no idea how to go about buying land or building a school, but I decided to take the plunge and use the donation money to build a small two-room school building behind Pastor Charles's church so that more children could be served. *Who knows how many more children I can enroll in school now that I can ask them questions myself in their own language?*

EIGHT

The Boy in the Pink Shirt

Gabriel: from the Hebrew name לְאִיתְבֵג *(Gavri'el)*
meaning "strong man of God." Gabriel was one
of the seven archangels in Hebrew tradition.[1]

W hile the showdown with Pastor Joe over the little girl's
horrific burn had been awful, my heart yearned to see
the children at Son of God Orphanage again. As often as I
could, I took the forty-five-minute tap-tap ride to visit them. I
began recognizing faces and names. I also began to realize that
cases such as the little girl with the infected burn were more
the norm than the exception. And although I never brought any
gifts or money with me as was expected, the director and his
wife allowed me to continue to visit.

After several visits on my own, I was surprised one day when
I stepped off the tap-tap from Gressier, only to see a huge tap-
tap parked in front of the orphanage. The front gate was ajar,
so I entered and heard a sound that shocked me and piqued my
curiosity. *English*. I heard many voices speaking English!

I tiptoed down the hallway and saw white skin. A large

group of Americans inhabited the back courtyard. Although I tried to enter unnoticed, someone spotted me at the top of the stairs and yelled out, "Hey there!"

"Hey," I answered back, as more than a dozen white people stopped what they were doing and stared at me. Then, just as quickly as they'd stopped, they turned back to singing, blowing bubbles, and playing games with the children. I felt as though I'd somehow entered the Twilight Zone. I walked over to the nearest white person, who was sitting on the steps, and asked, "Where are you from?" She told me they were from a church in the States, and they had been in partnership with this orphanage for two years. I walked down into the courtyard and enjoyed seeing the children getting some much-needed attention. Before the group left for the evening, I got their contact information so I could keep in touch. Finally, I wasn't alone.

But it turned out I never had been alone. Over the months of February and March, several more teams from several different states came to visit Son of God Orphanage. It was a consistent pattern that I had somehow missed during my first few visits to the orphanage, when I was always the only non-Haitian there.

From then on, each time a new team arrived, I would ask for contact information so I could keep the team updated about the orphanage. All the teams seemed to want to stay in touch, so they agreed to share their information with the strange, lone white girl who would randomly pop up at the orphanage. I also became friendly with the neighbors next door, and they would call me if they saw groups of foreigners enter the orphanage.

Then, less than a week later, I divinely connected with a wonderful woman from Colorado who would be leading a medical team on an upcoming visit. She explained in her e-mail that the doctors and nurses were coming to do medical evaluations of the children at the orphanage. On the day of their visit, I hopped in a tap-tap and arrived at the orphanage to jump in and start assisting the medical team, but immediately my inner antennae went up when I noticed something strange—dozens of children were being evaluated whom I had never seen in all my visits to the orphanage. I made a quick comment out loud, but one of the visiting team members shot back, quickly and decisively, "No. All of these kids live here." So I closed my mouth and kept doing what I was doing as more unfamiliar kids streamed through the pop-up clinic.

After a few hours I decided to take a break. The team's support members had set up a waiting area nearby where they played with children and kept them occupied until it was their turn to see the doctors. I sat on a step close to a pile of alphabet books, deep in thought, trying to make sense of all the confusion.

"Hi!" A woman with curly hair on the visiting team turned around and smiled at me. I smiled back. "I'm Rita. What's your name?"

She peppered me with all sorts of questions: "Who are you? Where are you from? Where do you stay?"

As I answered, I could tell she was more and more intrigued. Finally she looked me square in the eyes and said, "You know, I get a really strange feeling here."

My heart dropped at her words, and I felt my throat tighten.

She leaned in, asking quietly, "Do you?"

Unable to speak, I nodded my head slowly up and down.

She turned her head, looked to the side as if deep in thought, and said, "I just can't figure it out yet."

"Me either," I mumbled, a little in shock at her words because they mirrored my own feelings.

I looked away from the curly-haired woman to the doctors as a tiny boy waddled up to the examination chair. He had a distinctive pout on his lips, and I knew the doctors had seen him earlier that morning. "I think you've seen this little boy already," I said. No one seemed to be listening. I heard a halfhearted "Oh, really?" from someone, but nothing else happened. It wasn't a big deal, but I thought the team would want to know, for efficiency's sake. I was going to just let it go but then decided I had to try again.

I walked over, picked up the little pouting boy, and brought him to the curly-haired woman. "Excuse me," I said.

She glanced up.

"Rita, I think . . . well, I'm actually pretty certain we've seen this little boy already."

Rita listened; then we chatted for a second with some of the medical team, realizing that the orphanage director was sending the same children to the doctors but with different names in order for it to appear there were more children in the orphanage than there actually were. We sent the little boy off to play, and I let out a deep breath and returned to my work. While the rest of the afternoon was pretty routine, I still hadn't been able to determine what was causing these warning bells to go off in my spirit. Nevertheless, it felt like an incredible moment of success to connect with this one woman named Rita who cared and believed me.

As the team prepared to leave the orphanage, I asked, as I usually did, for contact information. I wanted to stay in touch with the team. Rita specifically came up to me before she left the orphanage and gave me her e-mail address, asking if it would be possible to be updated about the children.

A few weeks later, when the next team arrived at the orphanage, they decided to take the kids to Gressier for a day to run around on top of Bellevue Mountain. The city where Son of God is located is known as a concrete jungle. The sweet children at the orphanage never get to run in grassy fields, and most haven't even seen the beautiful Caribbean that is so close to them.

As this team loaded the children onto the rented tap-tap bus, I felt that familiar tug in my heart, the one I was becoming more and more accustomed to, so I decided to take one more look through the orphanage to see if we were missing anyone. As I stepped down from the bus, a few people called out, "We already checked" and "All the kids are here!"

"I'll be quick," I said. I ran back inside and hurriedly checked each room. When I stuck my head into the third room, I froze. There was a girl, in a pink T-shirt and no diaper, lying under a rusty bed frame and obviously not feeling well. I picked up the little, warm body and instantly realized I'd made a mistake. She was a *he*! As I rushed back onto the bus with the feverish little boy, I heard a few gasps.

"But I checked every room!"

"Me too. Where'd she find him?"

As I sat in my seat, someone handed me a diaper to put on the boy. Off we went to Gressier. Most of the kids were excited to be going somewhere, but Gabriel, the little boy in my arms, just lay there, warm, scratching, and coughing.

The kids ran around on Bellevue Mountain, playing, screaming, and laughing under the blue sky dotted with white puffy clouds. When they got hot and tired, they rested under the shady tree, but before long they were off again. While the visiting team played games with the kids, sang songs, and hung out, Gabriel lay in my arms that were now coated in his sweat. When we returned to the orphanage at the end of the day, I remembered the little burned girl and couldn't imagine sending Gabriel back inside in his current condition, so I asked Pastor Joe if I could take Gabriel to stay with me for a few days back in Gressier.

Pastor Joe did the usual shoulder shrug and nodded his head, murmuring, "Yes, no problem." His lack of care and indifference with the children had become increasingly evident to me, and it wasn't until later I realized how unacceptable my request of taking a child out of an orphanage without paperwork or proper approval really was.

That night I was staying at a guesthouse in Port-au-Prince, and that evening, as God would have it, an American doctor arrived. She came over and took a look at Gabriel for me.

"Bronchitis, scabies, and fungal infections, for starters," she pronounced. "This two-year-old is fighting hard. Here's some medication. Give it to him for seven days."

Children in Haiti suffer from all kinds of medical problems that many of us have never heard of. Scabies is one of those, a very contagious skin infection caused by a tiny burrowing parasite. It is extremely difficult to get rid of and causes intense itching, which gets especially unbearable at night.

In addition, bronchitis, usually very treatable in America, is a major problem in Haiti where respiratory conditions can be deadly, especially when combined with other untreated infections and chronic health problems. These are part of the reasons why Haiti has the highest infant and child mortality rates in the

Western hemisphere, with diarrhea, respiratory infections, and tuberculosis among the leading causes of death.[2]

Clearly Gabriel was very sick, and I was worried the orphanage wouldn't remember to give him his medication on time, so I called Pastor Joe, told him the diagnosis, and asked if I could watch him for the whole seven days to make sure he would get better.

"Yes. No problem," Pastor Joe said. I could picture the shrug.

Whew. Maybe with seven days of one-on-one care, Gabriel could get strong enough for his body to help fight off these infections. Bearing in mind Gabriel's condition, along with my misgivings about the orphanage now confirmed by Rita, I contacted the medical team that had just visited the orphanage and asked them to send their medical records to me. They agreed, and I started collecting information on each of the children in the orphanage.

By this time I had tracked over a dozen organizations that were supporting the orphanage and regularly sending in aid and food, but I had little evidence of those resources ever making it to the children. I had only been collecting information for a few months, but I realized that most of the organizations were unaware of the others that were supporting Son of God Orphanage. I sent out an e-mail to the list of leaders I'd compiled and requested they participate in a conference call so I could give them a briefing of what I'd been observing. With the assistance of a few close acquaintances who helped me coordinate, they all dialed in on the appointed day from four different time zones.

I understood that these good people who wanted to serve Haitian children might not want to believe a young girl they had never met, or perhaps had met only once. Especially if she was telling them that the resources they were allocating for the children at Son of God Orphanage were being funneled elsewhere. So I prayed right before the call that God would reveal to each person on the phone the truth of what was happening, and how each of them was a part of this, for better or for worse.

I began the call by introducing everyone who was on the line, then opened with a few examples of what I had observed at the orphanage. For instance, two of the organizations had given food to the orphanage nearly the same week, yet none of the children had been fed. There was silence on the line. I could almost hear alarm bells going off in people's heads.

My heart cringed as I heard that some of the groups had been working with this orphanage for more than two years, long before I had arrived. My heart broke even more as I learned that one particular organization had been regularly encouraging other churches to work with Son of God Orphanage. Their inexperienced leadership was constantly changing, and they seemed to be led more by their selfish desires than by any sense of accountability in following up on their charitable work. The more I saw this, the more I realized that some of the corruption in Haitian orphanages is a direct result of American churches and organizations who are well-meaning but who perpetuate the cycle of corruption and exploitation by donating without accountability. Sometimes these organizations tour orphanages, which unfortunately exist to show Americans how "poor and needy" their children are. Some orphanages, like Son of God, even purposely keep their children hungry and dressed in rags to attract more aid.

As the conversation ended, I could feel the tension and anxiety stirring up. Some of the leaders seemed a little more on fire, disturbed by what they had just heard but not sure what to do yet. And I did not have any clear answers or suggestions. All I knew was that I was there to observe and to call attention to what was going on. The information about contributions to the orphanage, along with medical records showing the poor health of the children, continued to pile up in my files.

As the Americans on the phone talked about some of the children they had seen or sponsored, their faces ran through my mind. When they spoke about a few children that I had never heard of, I realized that there had been many children at Son of God who were no longer there.

After the phone conversation, I compared the current lists of the children at the orphanage to older lists and discovered that children from Son of God Orphanage were going missing, and pretty consistently. *Where are they going? What has happened to these kids?* I knew I wouldn't be able to rest until I found the answers to those questions and uncovered more about what was going on behind the scenes at the orphanage, and with Pastor Joe.

NINE

A Dream Born Under the Tree

Although its main product may seem
like a rather minor food, tamarind
has been called a tree of life.
—From *Lost Crops of Africa*[1]

How is this real life? I found myself asking this question as I was standing on the balcony of a multimillion-dollar mansion belonging to one of my sister's friends. It had only been a few days since the conference call with the churches who sponsor Son of God Orphanage, and even though I was in West Hollywood to visit my sister, I couldn't stop thinking of all the poverty in Haiti.

A young man's voice snapped me out of my daydream. A fresh, nicely dressed guy named Kyle was talking to my sister, Lindsey. I edged forward to hear what they were saying, but they were talking about music and people I had never heard of.

Then Lindsey asked Kyle, "So what do you do now?"

"I build," he said. "I helped my dad build this house."

I looked around the room, feeling as though a lightning bolt had just zapped me. It was absolutely beautiful. I thought about the growing amount of kids in the dilapidated church and the need for a bigger school back in Gressier. Then I blurted out, before I even knew what I was saying, a strange invitation: "You should come and build my school in Haiti."

Kyle chuckled and asked me a few questions about Gressier and Respire Haiti. He gave me his information, and he didn't seem too alarmed when I said I'd e-mail him soon with more information about our organization and vision.

Before I knew it, I was flying back to Haiti. Lindsey had come along, and we faced a harsh transition from ritzy Hollywood mansions to no running water or electricity and the darned Haitian roosters who never really know the proper time to let loose their out-of-tune crows.

I had been living by myself for four months, and the Haitians probably thought I had no friends because there was a lot of curiosity when they saw Lindsey. The kids treated her like a celebrity, poking and prodding at her and calling her name relentlessly. She took it all in good humor. Monday morning, I took her to see the school. The new two-room school building behind the church was barely finished as we stood outside and peered in at the now one hundred or so children stuffed into the two classrooms. It was a wake-up call. Respire Haiti was already at full capacity with no room to expand, and there were hundreds of other children around the area who desperately needed to be in school. The Holy Spirit nudged me again, and I realized we were going to need a bigger school, and soon.

Lindsey stayed for two weeks, encouraging me and bringing laughter to the thickness of Haiti. She also helped me teach the English classes I had started in the afternoons a few days a week at the church. The classes had now grown to hundreds of children and adults.

At night we sweated our faces off under our mosquito nets, and the voodoo drums continued almost every night. Many nights I would look over, and my sister would be sound asleep, not even hearing the thump of the drums. It was so wonderful to have her with me and so hard to let her go.

I had heard plenty of horror stories about purchasing land in Haiti. And even though I had some funds now and could look into a land purchase, I had no idea if those funds would stretch to cover construction of a new, larger school. I also didn't know who would have the skills and experience needed to oversee such a project. Nonetheless, the tug in my spirit was too strong to ignore, so I began searching for land in Gressier.

I envisioned a new school built on flat land since I hailed from Louisiana, where everything is flat. But when Pastor Charles heard my idea for Respire Haiti's new school, he brought me to Bellevue Mountain. We stood together under the only tree on Bellevue Mountain, the one so many of our activities had been held under, and he said, "This land is for sale if you want it."

"Thank you," I said quickly, believing it would never work. "I know we hold our feeding program up here, but we need flat land. We can never build on this hill. The slope is too great."

Pastor accepted my answer and left it at that. I started searching again for just the right piece of land. For weeks I looked, finding a few flat pieces of property at ridiculously inflated prices.

Then, after not finding a flat piece of land I could afford, I caved in and agreed to purchase more than an acre on the top of Bellevue Mountain. It didn't cross my mind that the tree from my dream was right in the middle of the plot of land—my mind was already preoccupied with the problems of building on the steep slope.

A few weeks later Bret Pinson, from the church I had spoken at a few months earlier, came from Louisiana to Haiti and joined Bernard, Pastor and Madame Charles, and myself on the roof of my house as we reviewed the purchase contract written up by the local judge. Pastor Charles explained the terms to us, with Bernard there to translate for Bret. Everything was in order, so I took up my pen to sign the contract. When I finished, I looked up and was surprised to see that Pastor and Madame had choked up, with tears welling up in Madame's eyes.

Confused, I looked over at Bernard with a big question mark in my eyes, but he looked just as confused as me. *Should I be crying?* I wondered. *I know this is a big deal. Maybe I should be crying too.*

Then, as I watched and wondered, tears began to flow down both Pastor's and Madame's cheeks. Why? I had to know why they were so overwhelmed with emotion.

"Are you okay?" I asked Madame.

"These are tears of joy." She smiled.

I smiled back, nodding. I thought that was it. But she continued.

"We have been praying under that tamarind tree every Sunday at 4:00 a.m. for twelve years."

I could feel every bit of breath leave my body.

"We've prayed for God to send someone to come and transform this area," Pastor added. "We prayed for someone to build a school."

My eyes fell to the ground as I took in a breath, trying to gain the courage to look up at them without bursting into sobs myself. Finally I looked up, and my eyes met Madame's.

"We've been praying for you since you were twelve years old, Megan," she said.

Immediately I flashed back to my twelve-year-old self—bratty, smart-mouthed, and stubborn. "Wow," I gasped, as it began to sink in, and I caught a glimpse of how God was at work and why I had dreamed about the tree over and over. We all cried then and prayed, knowing God was doing something incredible.

The next night I woke up startled, feeling as though I'd forgotten something. I racked my brain, and all I could come up with was an urgent feeling that it was time to start building the new school up on the mountain. I tried to put the thought aside, but I couldn't seem to get back to sleep. Then Kyle, whom I had met in West Hollywood, came to mind. *Oh, yeah. I promised to send him an e-mail.*

I got up and sent a quick e-mail, asking if he remembered our brief meeting in Los Angeles. I timidly reintroduced myself and asked him if he might possibly be available to help begin building our school in the summer. Then I went back to sleep.

To my surprise, I received a response the very next morning. He seemed interested, and I gave him three pieces of information: I didn't have anything to offer except meals and a place to stay. I wanted to give him freedom to use his creativity, but he needed to use Haitian labor and materials. And I wanted to start as soon as possible. When I hit the Send button the second time, I didn't know what to expect. Kyle responded the next day. He was willing to come and check it out for himself.

I found out later Kyle canceled a trip to Europe to come to

Haiti and research building a beautiful, brand-new school for Respire Haiti up on Bellevue Mountain.

During the week of the land purchase, we decided to put up a fence, using the typical Haitian enclosure made of sturdy wooden sticks and barbed wire. A few neighbors had showed up to help dig holes when I heard a ruckus involving a man who had popped up out of nowhere. Everyone stopped working and stared as the man, who said he was a neighbor, complained about the fence. He started yelling about the wooden sticks blocking the road so he couldn't drive to the other side of the mountaintop.

"Do you have a car?" I kept my voice calm.

He shook his head no. I laughed inside, wondering why he was making a big deal about not getting a car up here when he didn't even own one.

A few minutes later Pastor arrived and began a conversation with the man. I went to the tamarind tree to rest in the shade. I watched the two men talking in loud voices and using lots of animated hand motions. *Things are always so complicated here,* I thought. Just as I let out a big sigh, Pastor came toward me. Behind him, I saw the angry man pick up a shovel and start digging a hole for the fence.

"What happened?" I asked Pastor.

"This man is a voodoo priest, and he wants to be able to get to the other side of the land because he uses it every Thursday night."

"How did you get him to pick up a shovel?" I was really confused now.

"I just told him that we would pay him to put up the fence if he wanted."

Pastor always seemed to know what to do in these situations, and I trusted his wisdom. As I watched the man, busy digging and carefully placing wooden sticks in the holes, I thought how ironic it was for a voodoo priest to be helping with site work for our Christian school.

My curiosity was sparked. I asked Pastor why the priest needed to get to the other side of the land on Thursday nights.

"Because that's where he does his voodoo ceremonies," Pastor said without hesitation.

"Seriously?" I retorted with a curious bewilderment.

Voodoo (also sometimes spelled *vodou*) is the main religion of Haiti, brought over by slaves from Western Africa and mixed with elements of the Taino Indians' religion and Catholicism. People who practice voodoo believe in the same God as Christianity, but they also believe in communicating with other spirits, who serve various roles in healing, casting spells, and more. Animal sacrifices and alcohol are both believed to give the *lwa* (Haitian spirits) rejuvenating power and the individuals involved in the ceremony favor. That's why bottles and blood are strewn across the ground after their ceremonies. Voodoo priests and priestesses always begin ceremonies by praying to God as the drums start up in the background, first slow and faint, then gradually louder and faster as the spirits come down to participate in the ceremony.

Without missing a beat, Pastor looked directly at me. "Yes, people come from all over the world to do voodoo, animal sacrifices, healing ceremonies, and more on this mountain. The past presidents of Haiti and many of the people in the government have come here."

I was puzzled, to say the least. *Then what are* we *doing on this land?* I wanted to say out loud. But all I could get out was, "Oh, okay," in a quiet murmur.

The fence was almost finished, and I was silent, completely stunned by the news I'd just received. I decided to head back down the mountain. As I walked alone and silent, Pastor's words kept spinning in my mind. *Why are people coming to do voodoo on this mountain? What is so special about it? What does this mean for us and for the school?*

Before I had any more time to really scare myself with my own thoughts, my sweet little neighbor Darlene ran up and grabbed my hand. As I looked down and smiled at her, my fear seemed to drain out a bit as I walked back home.

My short lease on my house was coming close to expiring, and I was becoming gradually more anxious about what to do next. One of my best friends from the States, Kathryn Davis had come to Haiti to spend the summer with me. I was so excited that we would be able to live together and love on the children of Haiti. Kat seemed to be less anxious than I was about the fact that we might be homeless in a few weeks.

As we discussed the complexities of finding housing in Haiti, especially in Gressier, where 75 percent of all the buildings were flattened by the earthquake a year earlier, my anxiety level grew. We decided to go for a run to relieve some of the stress. As we ran near Bellevue Mountain, we passed a man dressed in jeans and a polo. Kat nearly screeched to a halt and looked at me.

"You have to go ask him if he knows of any place for rent."

I laughed at her and kept running.

A few seconds later she laughed back and insisted, "I'm serious. Go ask him!"

I laughed a second time and replied emphatically, "No! I don't even know him. I'm not asking a stranger if he has a house to rent, especially here."

She shrugged and took a few more steps before grabbing my shoulders and loudly insisting, "Megan, the Holy Spirit is telling me that you need to talk to that man."

Feeling strange but somewhat backed into a hole, we made a U-turn with our running and ran up to the unsuspecting man. I approached him slowly, explained the situation of my contract being up for the current house I was in, and asked him if he knew of anything else available in Gressier. He chuckled and introduced himself as Marc, then motioned for us to follow him.

Looking at Kat, I had not yet decided if I wanted to punch her for making me talk to this man or hug her because she was right. Getting caught up in wondering where we were walking and if this was a waste of time, I nearly tripped over my feet as Marc came to a halt and pointed across the way.

I looked up to see the most beautiful, out-of-place house in Gressier, standing two stories tall, white, with two balconies, and an electrical pole in its front yard.

I looked over at Kat grinning from ear to ear.

"Electricity *and* water!" I excitedly told her. Even though I knew that both of these amenities would be extremely sporadic because of Haiti's poor utility infrastructure, I was still grateful for the possibility.

As Marc began explaining the situation of the house, the timing could not have been more perfect. Divinely, an organization was leaving in a few days, and the house could be ready for us when we needed it the next week.

My heart fluttered as once again God reminded me that He is the One organizing and planning every detail ahead of me, even when I might feel as though I'm walking on an unknown path.

TEN

Two Thousand Dollars

Apathy and evil. The two work hand in
hand. . . . Evil wills it. Apathy allows it. Evil
hates the innocent and the defenseless
most of all. Apathy doesn't care as long
as it's not personally inconvenienced.
—Jake Thoene

Gabriel's medicine worked, and over the next seven days at
my house in Gressier, the sick little two-year-old began
to feel better and get some energy. But he couldn't seem to sleep.
He spent every night screaming, fear and anxiety emanating
from his sweet body. It was clear something heavy was going on
although I wasn't sure what darkness he saw. A typical evening
for him meant screaming and wailing until all hours of the night
when, eventually, he would exhaust himself and lie down. Every
night I prayed over him, but sometimes that only made his crying worse.

When he would finally lie down on a mattress on the
ground, he would contort and scoot his body to the edge, then
off the mattress until he reached the cold, hard tile floor. Only

then would he begin to relax slightly and his tired body calm down. Every night without fail Gabriel followed this routine as if something plagued him. After he finished his seven-day course of medicine, I returned with him to Son of God Orphanage, hoping he'd be strong enough to continue his recovery alone.

But on an April visit, only a few weeks after he had been back in the orphanage, I snapped. Gabriel's condition was clearly worsening, and he was miserable, alternating between coughing fits and fiercely scratching every part of his body. I'm no doctor, but it was obvious he was suffering from scabies and fungal infections again. I could only imagine how awful it was for him to have his skin itching all over in the crazy Caribbean heat. Even after holding and kissing dozens of children who had scabies, I had never had the contagious skin-crawling disease, but I knew it was unbearable.

Once again I approached Pastor Joe and asked if I could take Gabriel home with me to Gressier to give him more medicine and the attention he needed. *Shrug.* His apathetic responses showed me he really did not care about this child who desperately needed help. *What kind of pastor is this?* I wondered yet again. I had recently discovered he practiced voodoo and began recognizing voodoo paraphernalia in the orphanage. The more I learned about Pastor Joe, the more his role as a pastor became tainted. I could see why the kids would flinch out of fear when he walked by, and many of them ran away when he was anywhere near. The stories the children would tell were haunting, and my spirit would lurch anytime I was near him. I felt as if there was an unmistakable darkness, not just in the orphanage but in him as well.

This time Gabriel stayed with me in Gressier for more than two months, and I was beyond excited to see real improvement.

I prayed over him continuously, as did my friends, and I could sense that as his health began to improve, his hard shell was melting, and he began to kiss rather than bite and accept a hug rather than turn away.

One day I received a phone call that Pastor Joe was in Gressier wanting to meet. I ran to the corner of a road where he was waiting for me. Curious, I asked what he needed.

"I need Gabriel back," he said, his voice a slur.

"Why?" I asked as my heart dropped. I really did want to know.

Shrug.

"Where is his family?"

"Dead." This was the standard answer Pastor Joe gave to anyone who asked about the families of the children in his orphanage.

This time I went a step further with my questions. "Do you have any paperwork? So I can keep him longer? Because he needs more attention to stay healthy."

And that's when the words came out, clear as day. I can still hear them in his brusque voice: "If you give me two thousand dollars, I will give you Gabriel." His eyes darted back and forth, as if making sure the coast was clear.

Confused and frozen in place, I stared at Pastor Joe. I couldn't get my thoughts organized. *What just happened?* I knew that was what he had come there to say. Finally my feet came unglued, and I walked away quickly, shouting back over my shoulder that we would talk later.

That night I prayed and cried and tried to process what had happened. I knew this was definitely not the way an adoption of a child should go. *Is he really selling me this child? Does he really expect me to give him money? What is going on?*

I racked my brain about who to go to for help. *There must be someone in Haiti who knows what to do.* Suddenly I remembered meeting a man with wise eyes named Jonathan. He worked for the Haitian Coast Guard. Since I was so new to Haiti, I didn't know any Haitian police officers I could trust, so this was as close as I could get to an official from whom I could get advice. I called him late that night as I stood on my roof, looking out over Gressier.

Jonathan listened but was puzzled at first. However, as we talked, and I told him the whole story about Gabriel and Pastor Joe's orphanage, Jonathan began to remember a training seminar he had attended that covered situations such as this one. All of a sudden he came alive, and his voice grew energized as he put the pieces together, and he said he would call me back in a few minutes. *Thank You, Lord.* I knew I needed help with this one.

Jonathan called back. He'd been busy making calls. And before I could catch my breath, it was like the pistol went off for a race. Jonathan had connections, and the people he called had connections, and before I knew it, meetings were planned, and organizations from Belgium, Germany, France, and Canada, along with Haiti itself, got involved. The consensus was that Pastor Joe had offered to sell me a child from his orphanage, and as more information surfaced about him and the number of children missing from Son of God, everyone involved realized this wasn't the first child he had sold, and he needed to be stopped. I agreed.

But what happened next really took my breath away. In order for Pastor Joe to be stopped from doing this to Gabriel or any other child again, he needed to be caught in the act of selling a child so he could be arrested and sent to prison. Because the child was offered to me, the plan organizers suggested I would be the best person to help carry out the sting. The plan terrified me, but it was the best and only option.

I remembered the first time I'd seen Gabriel in that pink shirt, all alone and sick as a dog in that room at the orphanage. I remembered his screams at night as he fought whatever darkness threatened to overwhelm him. And I remembered his first smiles and hugs when he began to feel better and safe. I wanted to do it but I was so afraid. *What is going to happen to Gabriel? What will Pastor Joe do if he finds out? Will I be safe? What if I have to leave Haiti because of this?*

The only thing I knew to do was pray. *Lord, please tell me what to do.* And here's how He answered—all I could think about were the countless other children this had happened to, and I knew I wasn't alone and that God would protect me. So I agreed to do it.

Over the next six weeks I met with the organizers of the sting, including Haitian officials. I told my story numerous times. I reviewed the Haitian laws that existed to protect children from trafficking.

Sometimes I felt as though I was part of an episode from *CSI.* At other times it seemed as if everything was unorganized, moving in different directions. Finally plans began to crystallize, and one Tuesday morning, when I happened to be in Port-au-Prince, I received a phone call telling me to be at the courthouse in twenty minutes. I looked at my watch. Even though I was less than a few miles away, in Port-au-Prince traffic that could mean an hour's worth of travel.

Kat and I both knew immediately what we had to do. We left the guesthouse where we were staying and walked out to the street. The fastest way to get to the courthouse would be to hire a motorcycle driver, so we stepped out onto the road to catch one. We tried to look for the most competent driver, but there were dozens whizzing by, and we would just have to pick one.

One young driver with a helmet on tapped his brakes and then motioned for us to hop on. I quickly explained that we were in a big hurry to get to the courthouse. I briefly negotiated the price, and he agreed to take us. Kat and I both climbed on and grabbed hold of the driver as he swerved in and out of traffic. Kat and I clung to each other and prayed no one would yell at us, or worse, as we drove through Cité Soleil, one of the largest and most dangerous slums in the world. I always tried to avoid it, but today it was the quickest way to get to the courthouse. We were making good progress through the winding streets and alleys when the moto suddenly slowed down. To our right a police officer stood in the middle of the street and was waving at us. *Uh-oh.*

We stopped and the officer motioned for us to get off the moto; then he asked our driver for his paperwork. He looked it over and threw his hands in the air, shouting at the driver that his paperwork was expired. Kat and I stood, helpless in the middle of a crowded Cité Soleil intersection, as I looked down at the minutes ticking away on my watch. My adrenaline kicked in, and I tried to swallow the rage rising from my gut.

I looked up at the police officer, who was shouting at the driver in Creole, "Get out of here!"

That wasn't going to happen. I reached one hand onto the back of the motorcycle, and stuck my other into Kat's hand. Then I looked straight at the angry police officer and said as calmly and clearly as I could in Creole, "We need the driver. He has to take us to the courthouse."

The police officer looked back at me, shrugged, and turned around. He mumbled to himself and shrugged again.

Suddenly I erupted, as if the Holy Spirit had lit me on fire, and I began sharing more information with him than he'd ever wanted to know. I shouted at the top of my lungs, in Creole in the middle of Cité Soleil, about Son of God Orphanage and that we had to get to the courthouse or else we would lose our chance to take care of a terrible problem that *must be stopped*! I yelled that the officer must not have children of his own if he was willing to let any child suffer.

I held on to the back of the motorcycle and told him, in no uncertain terms, that only this driver knew the way and he had to finish the job we had given him. When I finished, I took a deep breath and waited.

The police officer looked over at his partner, smiled at me, and said, *"Ou pale Kreyol tankou yon rat."* It's an odd compliment Haitians give that compares the person speaking Creole to a rat, but essentially it means, "You speak really good Creole."

I wanted to ball up my fist and shake it at him, but I wasn't letting go of the moto or Kat. I was annoyed but mustered a smile and spit out, "Thank you."

"Go, bring these girls," said the police officer to the moto driver.

Kat and I hopped back on the moto behind the driver. He began thanking me, but I rudely interrupted him. "Please don't talk. Just drive. Just get us there."

He fired up his moto, laughed, and took off. I held Kat's hand tightly in mine, and the sound of her singing in my ear soothed my raging heart.

Arriving at the courthouse, Kat and I ran into the building, looking disheveled from the wind blowing our hair and gray from the dirt that had pelleted our faces. Asking around for the judge, I was led down the hallway while the lights flickered on and off. Although it was only midafternoon, the place seemed to be deserted. I was led to a door where I knocked softly and heard a gruff, *"Entre."* Pushing the door open, I could see the look of surprise on the judge's face when he saw I wasn't Haitian. His mouth dropped open when I began explaining the situation in Creole. Amused, he asked intense questions about the situation of Son of God Orphanage.

Although he seemed intrigued and knowledgeable, there was no way to know if he would actually take the situation seriously. I left feeling as if I had been heard, but I was still anxious and unsure of what would happen next.

ELEVEN

They Don't Want Me

Home is a shelter from storms—all sorts of storms.
—William J. Bennett

Megan! Megan! Come see. Someone is here for you," my front-yard tent neighbor shouted. Feeling exhausted and a bit discouraged from my motorcycle ride to the courthouse the day before, I wasn't in the mood to hurry. I tried to see from the porch who was at my front gate, but the darkness and heavy rain made it impossible. I decided I'd better go check for myself, so I ran through the rain and pulled the gate open. I looked down, and there was tiny Michaëlle, soaking wet and looking exhausted. She was carrying a small wad of clothes in one hand.

"Michaëlle!" I said. "Hurry, come in."

What is she doing out so late and in the rain? I wondered as I brought her inside and dried her off. I wanted to shake my head as I looked at her frail, sickly body and wet clothes.

She was quiet and almost in a daze, staring at the ground. Finally she looked up at me. As long as I live I'll never forget what she said.

"Yo te di, ou ka pran mwen si ou vle . . . yo pa vle'm."

Shocked by her words, I wanted to make sure I understood her correctly and asked her to repeat it.

"They said you can take me if you want." Her small seven-year-old voice was flat and toneless. "They don't want me."

My heart felt as though it had fallen out of my chest onto the floor. My mind began spiraling, and my world changed in a blink as I looked into her eyes and held her hands. "They might not want you, but I do." I saw a slight smile. "You can live with me."

I knew what I was saying was not just a big step but a big life change. I didn't know how to legally adopt Micha; I didn't know if it would even be possible for a young, single American to do, so my decision to become her mother was ultimately a decision to stay in Haiti for the rest of my life or, at least, for the rest of Micha's childhood.

My mind went back several months to that first time I met Michaëlle on Bellevue Mountain, when she'd been so hungry she wanted to eat a bird. Ever since, she and a few other sweet girls had been spending the night at my house every Saturday night after the feeding program. It had become a precious time for them to get a bath and just be carefree little girls playing with their friends.

One Saturday in the early afternoon, I walked to her tent with a few other kids only to find her, sitting on a rough concrete block, surrounded by dirty dishes and a tub of milky white water. It looked as though the whole neighborhood had brought Micha their dishes to wash. I looked around to see who else was helping. Micha noticed my distress and bravely said, "No one else is here, but it's okay. I like to wash dishes." I remembered how much I'd hated washing dishes when my mom gave me the chore. The girls I'd brought sat down with me, and we began to help, scrubbing the pots and pans, lightening the load by splashing water and laughing together.

Over time I had begun to sense that Micha was changing, beginning to recognize the difference between right and wrong, between darkness and light. I had heard that she'd begun to stand up to the beatings, and it was killing me to know what was happening to her. When the people she lived with yelled at her and told her no one loved her or wanted her, she responded back, "Megan loves me. And Jesus loves me too." Evidently her aunt had heard it one too many times because this time she snapped, kicking her out and telling her, "Go find Megan."

I knew it wouldn't be easy. Now that Michaëlle would be living with me, I had to face directly all the abuse this sweet child had suffered and figure out how to walk with her through adjusting to a whole new way of life. But first, I needed to take care of the legal paperwork that would allow her to stay in my home.

After calling everyone I knew who might know the best way to do this legally, I got a tip to pay a visit to a judge in Gressier. Speaking with me briefly, he informed me that any living biological parents had to be present in order to complete any paperwork. From Michaëlle's previous living situation in the tent, I knew her father was alive. I searched for a few weeks and finally found someone who had a phone number for him. I called him, and he agreed to come to Gressier.

That morning still sits in a bit of a haze in my memory, as it seemed we raced all over Gressier. First, we visited the local judge and started some paperwork; then we were directed to other agencies and offices and finally ended up at the Gressier courthouse, where several officials in business suits sat outside under an overhang in plastic lawn chairs behind a folding card table. I approached slowly, trying not to look confused at their office situation, and began explaining Michaëlle's plight.

As I talked, Micha stared at the ground, embarrassed and scared. It was hard to hear the voices of the officials with the cars and tap-taps zooming along the National Highway behind me.

Next, they asked Micha to step forward and give her name. "Michaëlle," she said in a quiet voice. They asked her a question I couldn't quite make out with all the noise, but she turned, glanced at me with a beautiful, toothless grin, and said loudly, "Megan."

When her father was asked for her paperwork, he unfolded a torn and stained piece of paper, which turned out to be Micha's birth certificate. Next, he pulled a piece of torn notebook paper out of his wallet. I tried to glance over and read some of what it said, but it was in French. From the conversation I realized it was a death certificate for Michaëlle's mother, who supposedly died of a fever at home. There was no morgue where she lived, so she didn't have a proper funeral.

My heart throbbed with sadness as Micha stood, quietly listening to the questions the judge asked her father. "So you want to give your child away? You don't want to keep her for yourself?"

As he answered, Michaëlle moved closer to me and gripped my hand tightly. I prayed she would forget this feeling of being unwanted and instead be filled with the truth of how much I wanted her. Because her biological father could not read or write, the paperwork was read out loud to him carefully. As he verbally agreed to giving me custody of Michaëlle, he placed his thumb on an ink pad, then slowly pressed it to the paper. As he wiped his ink-stained thumb on his pants, he looked over at me with a grin that was identical to sweet Micha's.

Seconds later I heard, in English, "Congratulations!" As quickly as it began, it was finished. I shook my head as we walked away. I almost couldn't believe it. What a surreal moment, from the knock on the gate in the rain, to finding Micha's father, to petitioning the court at the card table in the outdoor office, this monthlong journey of getting custody of Michaëlle, the little girl I had met under the tree, was indescribable.

I felt an incredible rush of feelings as I tried to process what had just happened. *What did I just do? Will I be living in Haiti the rest of my life? Oh Lord, surely You would have given me a red light or boomed down in a loud voice or yelled at me to stop if this wasn't what You wanted.*

Yet when we parted ways with her father, I had the nagging feeling that in a perfect world, the story would have been much different. Her father would have the desire and the ability to keep his daughter. He would have rescued her after her pleas to him to be saved from her abusive situation in the tent on the mountain. He would have doted on her and loved on her, realizing her joy and her spirit are contagious. He would have told her she was smart and beautiful.

But the real world is hard, and the real world in Haiti is even harder. I struggled over the decision to adopt a child who actually has a father, but I could no longer justify a situation where a child was living with people who didn't want her, feed her, or keep her safe. I chose to rise above my anger over the unjust situation and trust that God knows Michaëlle and her past. He knows why things happen like this, even if I don't.

For weeks after she came to live with me permanently, my heart broke every time I'd drop something on the floor because she was immediately on her knees, cleaning it up. My mind is seared with the memory of the time I stepped in mud and she bent down and used her own shirt to wipe off my feet. Her sweet gestures were rooted in a corrupted idea of her role in this world. After her mother died, she was given over to another family to serve them, whatever that took, whatever that meant, and with no one to protect her.

Slowly, though, her sweet spirit began to break through the protective shell of anger that had formed around her. The darkness she'd been exposed to was being replaced with light and truth. And at the age of seven, she was finally learning how to color with crayons, how to play, and how to be held and hugged.

Not long after I became Micha's mother, a group of Americans came to Gressier to visit Respire Haiti. Back then, it was unusual to have visitors. It was even more unusual when they asked to do a skit and a Bible story at the two-room school. But Rita Noel, whom I had met at Son of God Orphanage a few months earlier, wanted to visit Gressier, Bellevue Mountain, and the school. But when they arrived, I second-guessed myself, thinking anxiously, *These kids aren't used to visitors . . . or Americans.*

I had already been into the church school once to give a warning speech to the students: "Please don't yell at the top of your lungs. Please don't ask for their electronics or the pieces of jewelry you see. Please don't stab each other with pencils. Please be good." *Whatever that meant.*

I held my breath as the team of fifteen entered the makeshift classroom, and I winced as I saw a few students reach out into the aisle to touch the side of a white leg or a white arm. The visitors performed a skit about putting on the armor of God, and I was delighted to see the children's eyes glued to the presentation. One of the team members, a cute guy named Josh Anderson, wore a vest made out of a paper bag and a Burger King crown on his head. The kids laughed and seemed to love every moment. After the skit the children went from station to station, making their own armor of God. My heart filled with joy.

After about an hour at the school, the team headed back to my house for peanut butter and jelly sandwiches. During lunch, someone asked about the land up on the mountain: "Is that where you are going to build your school?" I responded that it was, and they all wanted to see it. So I led the group across the road and along the winding path through the mango trees, where the goats grazed in the weeds. As we slowly began the arduous uphill walk to Bellevue Mountain, one of the men started running up the hill backward. "Spring training," he shouted, as we all laughed, and he picked up his pace.

Up on top of Bellevue Mountain, I explained the importance of this land, that people from all over the world and Haiti have come here for years to perform animal sacrifices and a plethora of voodoo ceremonies. The group listened intensely as I showed them the remains from a ceremony the night before, broken glass and white powder. Then everyone spread out to pray; we breathed in the fresh air and looked out toward the waters of the Caribbean. I stood between Rita and Josh, and we linked our hands and lifted them high, offering my plans for the school to the Lord. After we finished praying, the backward-running guy approached and talked to me about Respire and the school. He was a huge man, towering over me, but I was caught up in his heart for children, for education, and for the future school. I thanked him for the encouragement as we headed back down the mountain.

Back at the house, someone came up and said, "Do you know who you were just talking to?"

"Some sweaty guy who loves Haiti?" I laughed.

"His name is Adam Hayward, and he plays football for the Tampa Bay Buccaneers."

I laughed out loud again, thinking about his "spring training" up the mountain. I thought he'd just been kidding. I also thought about how wearing shorts and a T-shirt and sweating in the Haitian sun makes everyone look pretty much the same. There are no superstars here; we're all just servants.

TWELVE

The Sting

Speak up for those who cannot
speak for themselves.
—Proverb 31:8 NLT

I woke up that morning listening to the now familiar noises outside my window—children's voices, people walking by to get water or take their children to school, and roosters crowing to greet the sun. Then it hit me. *Today's the day.*

The months of meetings, plans, and courthouse visits were over, and I felt a surreal sense that the final piece of the puzzle was about to be set. *Today it's all going to happen. Lord, be with me. Be with Gabriel. Be with us all.*

One last time I climbed up into a tap-tap with Gabriel and rode to Son of God Orphanage. I knocked on the gate and was led into the all-too-familiar waiting room. As soon as Gabriel recognized where he was, he buried his face into my chest and clung so tight his nails were digging into my arms. As we waited, Gabriel squirmed in my lap, anxious to leave, and my heart beat so fast I thought I might hyperventilate.

Not many of the adults at the orphanage really knew I spoke

Creole, so I brought a translator, Nathanial, with me. In fact, a few weeks earlier he and some of the detectives had blended in with a visiting team to secretly inspect Son of God Orphanage. As we walked through the orphanage, Pastor Joe pointed out the empty cupboards and the need for food while I quietly directed their eyes to where they hid the food and other supplies. Although I had only met Nathanial a few times, I liked him; he was a huge, friendly man with a serious face and kind eyes that seemed to constantly reassure me.

Pastor Joe walked in and sat down across the coffee table from me. He had an arrogant smirk on his face and immediately asked in Creole if I'd brought the money. He never even looked at Gabriel.

Nathanial translated, and I nodded slowly. Then he asked again, and I realized he wanted to see the cash. I pulled the bulging envelope out of my bag, remembering what the team had warned. "Don't let him grab it. And don't give it all to him at the same time."

Holding the envelope in both hands, I asked Pastor Joe to confirm the arrangements. "Are we leaving right away to go meet Gabriel's family and get his paperwork?"

Pastor Joe nodded his head in affirmation, then stuck out his hand for the envelope. I pulled the stack of money out and began to quickly count it into his outstretched hand. When I'd given him half, I put the rest back inside the envelope and shoved it down into the bottom of my purse. "You'll get the rest when we get there," I said, releasing a deep breath. I was shaking as I waited for his reaction.

Pastor Joe shrugged and stood up, waving for us to follow him outside. Nathanial stood up first, and I followed. Outside,

Pastor Joe turned to me, pointed to his car, and asked, "Do you have any money for gas?"

I had expected this request and had a twenty-dollar bill ready in my pocket. As I pulled the money out, Pastor Joe grabbed it and shoved it in his pocket. He opened the door and climbed in the driver's seat. Nathanial opened the back door for me, and I awkwardly worked my way in, Gabriel's head still buried in my chest. While I was getting us settled, Gabriel peeked up at Pastor Joe, and his eyes shot wide open in fear. I heard a small whimper from him; then I covered his face with my hand and gave him a gentle hug.

Pastor Joe yelled, and before I knew what was happening, a tall, lanky young man jumped in the backseat with me. I had no idea who he was but figured out he was asked to tag along so Pastor Joe wouldn't be by himself. He smiled at me, and I tried to smile back, but I could see his eyes reflect my own confusion and fear, and he turned to look out the window. He probably wished he was somewhere else. So did I.

As Pastor Joe started the car, I began to pray in earnest. At first I felt peace, knowing I'd been following God's leading in all this. *God, I know You have a better plan for the children in this orphanage.* But as we drove, my worry and fear began to rise and dissolve my quiet confidence. I was scared and confused. *I am an idiot for doing this,* I thought. *What was I thinking? Am I doing the right thing?*

I thought about the police officers, government agency officials, and international task force members who were involved. We'd planned the operation out carefully, but it was my neck and Gabriel's on the line right now. The thoughts came hard and fast now, flooding my mind as we bumped along. *What if everything goes wrong? Does Pastor Joe suspect anything? What if he figures out what I'm doing and why? What if he attacks me? Am I going to die today?* I thought about sweet Micha, who was at my house in Gressier with my friend Kat. I breathed in deep and began praying again. *Lord, You are in control. Please give me the peace that surpasses all understanding,* and I felt it—the same peace that had carried me through the last six weeks of planning this day.

Pastor Joe pulled the car onto the highway, and as he accelerated, he reached into the back pocket of his pants and pulled out an object I couldn't quite see. I heard a *clunk* as he dropped it on the center console. I looked down in horror. It was a handgun, the barrel pointing toward the dashboard. I stared at the gun, my arms tightening around Gabriel. Fear rose up again as I began praying over him and over us. Once again I felt God's presence, reminding me, *You are not alone. I am with you.*

I closed my eyes and rehearsed the plan again in my head. *You will pass through a police checkpoint. The police will pull us over and ask Nathanial to get out of the car. Nathanial will hesitate. Then the police will ask everyone to exit the car.* It seemed simple enough.

But when I opened my eyes, I saw a road chock-full of cars, tap-taps, motos, and people walking. A typical Haitian traffic jam. Pastor Joe let out a loud, annoyed grunt, slowed down, and pulled to the side. Then he yanked on the wheel, turning the car around in a cloud of dust, and stomped angrily on the gas pedal.

No. No! I wanted to scream, the words fighting to pour out of my mouth. *This is* not *the plan. This is not the route. This is not the way!* I fought against a scream as I realized we were going to miss the checkpoint. I looked up at Nathanial in a panic, and he began asking Pastor Joe, in a calm and quiet voice, why we had turned around. "The way we were going was the best way," Nathanial said.

"Yes," Pastor Joe said, "but I don't want to sit in traffic." Fortunately traffic was terrible in this direction, too, and it wasn't long before he grunted again and made yet another U-turn, pointing us back in the original direction. *Whew*. I breathed out in relief. *That was close.*

We picked our way through the traffic, and before long I saw the police checkpoint in the distance. The Haitian police officers were in their usual dark uniforms, big and burly, with shiny reflective sunglasses on. I looked out my window and saw a familiar face, an officer who'd met with us the night before for one last preoperational briefing. Just as we were about to roll up, he turned his back to the cars, plugged his left ear with his finger, and listened intently to the cell phone held up to his right ear. We kept rolling. *Are they not going to stop us?* I wanted to bang on the window and shout or throw something at him. *You're supposed to stop us, and your back is facing us. You are going to miss us! What am I going to do?*

I tried to hold down my panic, and as we drove by, I turned my whole body around to look out the back window. Nothing. The officer was still turned around, still on the phone. Just as I turned back around in complete despair, a man wearing an orange safety vest stepped in front of our car, waving his arms and pointing to the side of the road. Pastor Joe grunted again, pulled over, and stopped the car. Nathanial's door flew open, and he exchanged words with the man in the vest. They began shouting, and I covered Gabriel's ears with my hands. The police officer bent down and looked at all of us inside the car. "Where are you going?" he asked in a loud voice. I said nothing. My job was to be silent and look afraid; both were extremely easy for me to do.

Next, the police officer yelled at Pastor Joe. "Get out of the car!" He didn't wait for Pastor Joe to move but bent down and reached over him to grab the gun from the console. Pastor Joe, outraged at both the traffic stop and losing his gun, yelled back at the officer. "What is the meaning of this? What is happening?"

The police officer searched Pastor Joe's pockets and quickly found the wad of hundred-dollar bills. "What's this for?" he demanded.

"For my church," he said. "I am a pastor."

"Oh. A pastor with a gun on the console and a child in the car," said the officer with a smirk. "Okay." He turned toward the car and yelled at the lanky young man in the backseat to get out of the car too. "Who are you? How do you know this man?" he demanded, but the boy, clearly terrified, mumbled something about him just being asked to come along for a ride.

Next, the police officer pointed at me, still inside Pastor Joe's car with Gabriel. He waved for me to get out, and I scooted over and climbed out, clutching Gabriel for dear life. The officer pointed to me, then to a car with tinted windows, and shouted, "You! You need to go over there now."

I looked at Pastor Joe, relieved that I would have some space between myself and him. I was still afraid he might figure out what was really happening. He noticed my stare and, thinking I was looking for his permission to move, tilted his head and told me to do what the officer said: go over to the other car.

I walked with Gabriel to the car with the tinted windows. The back door popped open, and I saw familiar faces inside. I jumped in the car with Gabriel and quickly shut the door. Then

I watched out the window as the police arrested Pastor Joe, cuffing his hands behind him. His face registered a mix of surprise and fury as he kept talking in a loud voice, trying to explain that he was a pastor and he was on a very important errand. Tears ran down my face, and the others in the car said something about me doing a good job, but all I could do was pray that we were almost finished.

I looked at the official nearest me and asked, in confusion, "Can I go home now?" I'd forgotten the next part of the plan.

"No," he answered. "We have to go to the police station now, remember?"

As we took off for the police station, I stroked Gabriel's cheek. *This is all for you and for the other children,* I thought. They'd been through hell with this man.

We had concluded, after dozens of visits with careful observation and comparing records with the organizations that supported Son of God Orphanage, that Pastor Joe had set up the orphanage as a business, with the children as the product. Joe had made the rounds of poor neighborhoods, presented his services as a provider of a safe place for children to live, and set up his facility. The orphanage was run-down and lacking beds, latrines, plumbing—just about anything that would make it functional for so many children to live there.

But American churches had come to the rescue, raising money, collecting donations, and hopping on flights to bring clothes and food to the poor, sick, orphaned children. Teams typically spent five days in Haiti with the children, handing out clothes and food, and then leaving, feeling they had really helped, when in reality Joe would hide and later sell all the donations. The organization that continued to introduce churches and groups to Son of God Orphanage seemed continuously misguided. The leadership of that organization changed frequently, and the team leaders were extremely young and inexperienced. It was apparent that no one really picked up on or addressed the red flags along the way. All this confusion proved that the "savior" mentality of many Americans can blind people to real evil that is happening.

It was only after I had started visiting the orphanage consistently that anyone discovered all was not as it seemed. Clothes? Gone. Toys and games? Missing. Food and medicine? Gone after a day or so, when the children would return back into their ragged clothes and lethargy would set in again because they were hungry.

A week or two later the cycle would start all over. A new church group visits, not knowing about the previous one. More food, clothes, toys, and medicine to save the children at Son of God Orphanage. And once again it's all gone within a few days after the team leaves. For Pastor Joe, children equaled money in his pocket. And even worse, in the few months I'd been visiting the orphanage, more than fifty children went missing, and I didn't know where they had gone.

But I did have Gabriel, safe in my lap. We were almost at the police station. And, hopefully, we'd be finished soon and on our way back home, never to see Pastor Joe again.

THIRTEEN

The Start of Everything

If you do it with love, you can't mess up.
—Father Blessing

At the police station I was asked to empty my purse, my pockets, everything. I did what they said, trying to look scared. And once again, I didn't have to act; I was truly feeling it.

A moment later the police escorted Pastor Joe inside. That's when I remembered the plan—we were both going to be arrested and questioned, a ruse so that Pastor Joe would not know who turned him in for selling children. As far as he knew, I was in trouble for *buying* a child. They sat me down in a nearby waiting room, Gabriel still on my lap. Pastor Joe followed and was told to sit next to me. "He is the last person I want to sit next to right now," I wanted to scream.

A police officer looked at me sternly. "What happened?" he asked.

Seriously? I thought, confused. *What am I supposed to say?*

"What happened?" the officer repeated louder.

"Nothing," hissed Pastor Joe.

The officer pulled out a plastic bag with the wad of hundred-dollar bills inside. "Obviously, this isn't nothing!" he yelled.

Pastor Joe looked at the ground. The police officer looked over at me. "Who is that?" he asked, pointing to the child on my lap.

"Gabriel," said Pastor Joe.

"Gabriel who?"

Pastor Joe looked at me, puzzled. I returned his stare, equally confused, and then I felt a quick flash of anger. *You don't know his last name. You were about to sell me a child from your orphanage, and you don't even know his last name. Sick.*

The officer walked out, and more police arrived, some of their faces familiar. *At last,* I thought, and breathed deep. The new group of police officers began to argue loudly with the officers at the station, wondering why Pastor Joe and I were being questioned in the same room. I had seen enough television shows to know that wasn't exactly the correct procedure. The next thing I knew, Gabriel and I were being whisked away to another room. My possessions were returned to me in a plastic bag, and, relieved, I thought my time was over as they led me down a hallway and sat me in a chair outside the common holding cell, full of people. I tried not to turn around because I didn't want to see the hands sticking out between the bars. The gray walls were greasy, and the stench from inside was revolting.

The men inside were directing comments my way. "I haven't seen my family in three days," said one. "They don't know where I am."

"I've been in here for nine days, and they haven't even told me why," said another man. On and on it went, the desperate men inside the locked cell, trying to plead their cases to the back of my head. My heart hurt, thinking about the injustices locked up in that tiny, dark, five-by-five-foot space.

Finally I couldn't take it any longer and grabbed some granola bars from my purse to silence their pleas. "I'm so sorry. I really can't help right now," I whispered in Creole, holding out the granola bars. As the hands frantically grabbed at mine, the police officer sitting at his desk down the hall realized that spot was probably not the best place for Gabriel and me to sit. He walked over, and after I stood, he picked up the chair and moved me to a corner away from the holding cell.

We sat and waited. Minutes turned into hours, and Gabriel fell asleep on my shoulder. I waited, smelling the men in the holding cell and listening to their occasional listless comments. Finally an officer yelled at me to follow. I got up from my chair with a now very grouchy and exhausted two-year-old and was led down the hall and out a door to another car. "Where are we going?" I asked.

"To the orphanage," someone shouted from behind.

"What? Why are we going to the orphanage?" I asked, but no one listened, and we were hustled into the car. A man hopped in the front seat, and we zoomed away at the head of a caravan of cars. When the line of cars pulled up in front of the orphanage, I was one of the first out of the car. Approaching the gate, I thought I heard something strange. *Is that . . . music?*

A group of people followed behind me. Suddenly someone bulldozed his way to the front. My mouth literally dropped open as I saw Pastor Joe approaching. I was told I wouldn't have to see him again, and here he was, pushing his way through people to open the gate of the orphanage. He looked exhausted and angry. He furiously swung the gate open, and the officers and I followed him down the dark, narrow concrete hallway. *I do hear music. And . . . cheering?*

I was completely confused when we emerged into the back courtyard to the sounds of children yelling and cheering. "My father's coming! My father's coming!" their voices rang out. I'd never heard anything like that on any of my visits.

I looked around in complete disbelief. Balloons and streamers filled the dusty courtyard. Benches and chairs I'd never seen before were lined up around the edges. It was a surreal moment, and I looked around at the orphanage kids playing card games, playing bingo, and coloring with crayons. They were wearing newer, nicer clothes. The kids I'd seen with burns on their arms and legs wore long-sleeved shirts and pants to cover up their scars. The children with fungal infections on their scalps were wearing hooded sweatshirts.

I just stood, looking around for a few minutes and then, pinched myself, literally, thinking it was a bad, sick dream. I had visited this place dozens and dozens of times and had never seen anything like this before, even when American teams had been visiting.

Investigators came in and questioned the workers, once again not separating anyone. "Do the children eat? Do they like it here? Are they beaten?"

The answers were the same, sounding carefully rehearsed. "Yes, they eat. No, they are not beaten. Yes, they love their father, Pastor Joe."

Then they questioned the children while the workers watched their responses like hawks.

I felt sick.

My eyes landed on one sweet little girl named Sarah. I had cleaned her wounds so many times, and now she looked up at me, her eyes hollow and defeated. "Hi," I whispered. She half smiled, then turned her eyes away quickly.

Investigators and official observers were milling around, and I overheard them remarking on how sweet and nice the orphanage was. I couldn't take it any longer and stormed out, full of confusion and anger at how the sting was turning out. I could feel the acid coming up my throat and couldn't hold it back anymore. It felt as though evil was winning. I made it just outside the gate, put Gabriel down on the ground, and began vomiting.

What happened? What went wrong? I wondered. *How many of these people understand what is happening here? Do they* want *to cover up the abuse and the darkness of this orphanage?* I could not understand it.

I remembered previously, during a few of our large meetings, receiving texts from some of the lead investigators that showed their suspicion of corruption. I would open the text in the midst of a meeting about Son of God and read, "The man in the yellow shirt on your left is part of it." Or "The man on the right in the blue shirt is trying to cover up his role in this scam." I had known there was corruption, but I honestly didn't think that we'd go this far and hit a wall.

Now I didn't know what to do or where to go. I couldn't go back inside, so I decided to wait by the car. Then I saw him—one of the head investigators. Afraid of what I had just seen but still somehow bold, I walked right up to him and began telling him the truth. "This orphanage has never looked like this before. Someone obviously knew we were coming."

"Well, we took away Pastor Joe's phone," he replied confidently.

I said it again, my certainty growing. "They *knew* we were coming. This place has *never* looked like this."

Something in my voice seemed to get through to him, and he looked as if he actually believed me. "Are you sure?" he asked.

"Not only am I sure; I am positive. I have many people who will tell you the same thing!"

The investigator turned away and made a few phone calls. Suddenly police officers, investigators, and officials began pouring out of the gate and piling into the cars to head back to the police station. I let out a deep breath, got into the car with Gabriel, and wondered what was going to happen next. So far, almost nothing was going as we had planned.

Within minutes of arriving back at the police station, someone walked up to me, said, "Thank you so much," and began pulling at Gabriel, trying to take him away from me.

"What are you doing?" I was exhausted, confused, scared, and angry, and now *this*.

"The boy has to come with us now," the voice said, trying to lift Gabriel up and out of my arms. I instinctively tightened my grip and backed away. Gabriel began to whimper and wail, then quickly launched into full-blown screams.

"He needs to go with us so we can do our paperwork," a man said coldly, and then without any hesitation, reached over and violently ripped Gabriel out of my arms. I watched as Gabriel's eyes filled with fear and his screams intensified.

Someone opened a car door, and the man holding Gabriel put him in the backseat, shut the door, and went back inside the police station. Tears were streaming down my face as I stood there, waiting for someone to notice and to help. But there was no one. Gabriel was banging on the window at the glass separating us, still screaming.

I was considering opening the door and grabbing him out of the car to take him back when the man came back outside—shouting over Gabriel's cries and my pleas. "We need to take him," he said again harshly.

I melted. My courage and calm and peace and trust were all gone. My legs gave out, and I fell to my knees as the car pulled away with Gabriel. Some of the observers who'd been part of planning the sting came to me and lifted me up off the ground. Someone brought around a car to take me home, and as I got inside, I began to cry and scream, too, about how I would never see Gabriel again because I knew the corrupt officials were going to hide him from me.

The driver looked back at me and said quietly, "You will see him in five or six days. He will be okay." But I knew he was lying, and my heart exploded in sorrow and anguish. I sobbed all the way home.

I dragged myself into my house, completely exhausted emotionally, physically, and spiritually. I collapsed in bed, with Micha curled up next to me, crying myself to sleep with my Bible in my arms. I could not believe what had just happened. It had been the longest and most heart-wrenching fourteen hours of my life.

It seemed like the end of everything. Nothing had gone according to plan. I'd been so afraid Pastor Joe would figure out who was behind the sting operation and that he would attack or even kill me, but nothing like that had happened. Instead, the attack came when I thought everything was over and we were safe. But we weren't safe. Gabriel wasn't safe. Now he was gone, and I wasn't sure what to do next. But I knew I could never return to the orphanage.

The next day I got word that Pastor Joe had officially been arrested and was awaiting sentencing. But because the charade of nicely dressed children happily playing in a decorated courtyard had worked, the orphanage was going to stay open for business. Pastor Joe's wife would be running it while he was in jail.

I felt sick to my stomach, and I knew the sting had not ended anything. Instead, it highlighted the undeniable corruption and confusion that revolves around child rights in Haiti. I knew that this was only the beginning of bringing the darkness to the light. I wasn't going to let evil win.

Michaëlle standing on Bellevue Mountain, the first time I ever saw her, January 2011

Gabriel and me standing inside Son of God Orphanage, March 2011

Amanda Truxillo

Our family, November 2013

August 2011, the first time Michaëlle (standing) and Jessica (sitting) met after who knows how long

Teaching my English class in the
dilapidated church, March 2011

Enjoying some time with my sister, Lindsey,
on her first visit to Haiti, April 2011

Adam Hayward, Washington Redskins
linebacker, at Son of God Orphanage
during his June 2011 visit

HANNAH MCKENZIE

Walking and praying over the land on Bellevue
Mountain, May 2011, before I purchased it

Kat, Bernard, and me painting classrooms during the Christmas break and getting them ready for our move-in date

Jessi White Morris, Rita Noel, me, and Kyle Fishburn in the future home of Respire Haiti Café

Kyle and me working together on our first building

JOSH ANDERSON

Construction on our first six-classroom building

Michaëlle and me on that first day

Michaëlle's incredible transformation into a precious seven-year-old, one month after she started living with me, July 2011

REGINA ANDERSON

Tachi, one of my best friends and the manager of the Respire Haiti Café, with her beautiful daughter, Esther

Students walking up the pathway
to Bellevue Mountain

Respire Haiti Christian
School opened its doors
exactly one year after
I moved to Gressier

Respire staff praying over our students
that first day, January 9, 2012

Our first field trip, June 2012

The sign to Respire Haiti's mountain

Jessi White Morris

Walking four girls to class who
had never been to school

Melissa Breedlove Photography

Feeding program on Bellevue Mountain, November 2011

JESSI WHITE MORRIS

Josh's proposal, November 2012

My uncle T-tone, walking me down the aisle on Bellevue Mountain, January 2013

My mom with Josh, Micha and Jessi, and me at our wedding reception

Breaking ground on the Love+1
Medical Clinic, September 2013

High School students walking to
their new classrooms, January 2013

The tamarind tree on Bellevue Mountain

Worship on the last day of school, Bellevue Mountain, June 2014

FOURTEEN

Deux Enfants

However motherhood comes to you, it's a miracle.
—Valerie Harper

Just days after the sting operation, I watched Micha close her eyes one night as her body relaxed snug in her bed, and she began to drift off to sleep. Her eyes popped open one last time, and she looked at me as she cuddled her pillow. I smiled at my precious daughter who had been living with me for barely a month. She smiled back, half asleep, and murmured, "Look, there's room in my bed for another child."

I stroked her soft cheek, laughed off her comment, and said, "Time to get some sleep, Micha." But as I walked out of the darkened room, I felt a quick, deep pang, as if something important was missing.

A few minutes later I was relaxing outside in the backyard for a rare moment of quiet. I gazed at the Haitian night sky, so bright with stars. I smiled as I thought of Micha safely asleep in a soft, comfortable bed. For most of her life she'd been forced to sleep on a cardboard box under the kitchen table and, sometimes, even on the ground outside the blue tent.

Then her words came back to me. It was probably just an impulsive thought from a sweet, little seven-year-old girl, but I kept thinking about her words and couldn't seem to let them go. Maybe there was something more to what she had said.

I hopped up and went back inside the house. I pulled open the drawer where I kept Micha's paperwork. I had to look at her custody papers again. I unfolded a torn-up piece of loose-leaf paper and sat down to look. I started sweating, anxious and afraid for some reason. Again and again in my head I replayed the day I had received the death certificate for Michaëlle's birth mother.

The day I received custody of Micha, I'd been given the paper and immediately put it away for safekeeping. It had seemed so fragile, as if it might dissolve right there in my hands. I had never read it because it was in French, the language of the courts and the government in Haiti. I had taken a little French in high school but didn't remember enough to translate what the paper said. I had honestly never really thought about actually trying to read what it said.

But now I felt compelled to decipher it the best I could. Struggling over the faded letters, I tried to sound out the words using my French dictionary. I sighed. *Why, oh why, didn't I pay attention in French class?* I sighed again, still sweating and feeling anxious. Then one sentence jumped off the paper and into my mind: ". . . *Elle mort dans le presence de son mari avec deux enfants.*"

I knew *enfants* meant children, and *deux* was two. After consulting my dictionary for the rest of the words, I spliced together the whole sentence. ". . . She died in the presence of her husband and two children."

Wait. Two children? Two. Two?!

My emotions, already stirred up, were now supercharged, and a million questions flooded my mind. *Micha has a brother or a sister? Where is he or she? What happened? When were they separated? Why hasn't she talked about this before?*

Sleep was impossible that night. I tossed and turned with the excitement and the fear I had about Micha having a sister or brother. One question in particular haunted me. *Is she or he still alive?*

The next morning the same tumultuous feelings and questions woke up with me. I prayed about what to say to Micha, and I knew my heart wouldn't let me wait. Within minutes she was awake too. In the most calm and gentle way I could muster, I looked at Micha and asked, "Do you have a brother or a sister?"

Her eyes squinted a bit as if she was trying to awaken something from deep in her memory. I held my breath while she turned her head from side to side, looking around with eyes unseeing and still not saying anything. I held my breath and waited. Finally she answered.

"I think so," she said slowly, looking up at me with wide eyes.

My heart leapt out of my chest. I asked her a few more questions, to see how sure she was, and got much of the same uncertain response.

I had kept Michaëlle's biological father's phone number, so I decided the next step was to call and ask him directly. I had to. I felt like I was holding my breath again while the phone rang. He answered the phone, and I asked, "Does Michaëlle have a brother or sister?"

"Wi. Yon ti sè."

A little sister!

I knew the question I wanted to ask next, but I was afraid,

my heart beating like crazy. I wasn't sure where this would lead. I finally forced out the words in a rush.

"Do you know where Michaëlle's sister is?"

He hesitated too. Then rambled, "I don't know where she is, but I can try to find out."

My words flew out faster than I could push them back in. "Please find her so she can come here and grow up with her sister."

He agreed, and while I heard excitement in his voice, he said he didn't know for sure where she was living. We hung up, and I tried to swallow back the tears. My head and heart have always fought this internal battle regarding adoption. From the very first time I learned Michaëlle's story, I had a strong desire to help her escape the abusive situation she was in and then reunite her with her father. But that naïve fantasy changed when Micha stated bluntly that her dad had visited her several times and she had begged him to rescue her from the abuse. He listened to her pleas but had always gone away, leaving her there.

Michaëlle's story had engraved itself on my heart as God started chiseling away my closed-minded stance that children with living biological parents should not be adopted. The more I'd prayed about this, the more God had given me peace, and I heard Him saying, *She tried to tell her father, Megan. You've tried to explain her situation to him too. This child, Megan, is now your daughter.*

In my heart of hearts, I knew her biological father could not give Michaëlle what she needed—food, safety, a chance to go to school. It broke me, but I understood that was why God brought us together that first day near the tree on Bellevue Mountain.

For the next month I waited and prayed for the calmness and the patience to let God do His work. I also prayed God would help Micha's biological father find her sister and a way to get her to our house safely. God answered those prayers by protecting my heart, and Micha's heart; so much so that though it took weeks, it seemed like only days when I received a call from Bernard. I barely had the chance to say *Bonjou* before Bernard rattled off something about how a little girl who looked so much like Micha was sitting on my front porch. Micha and I were running an errand. I looked over at her sitting next to me in the car and smiled, barely keeping back the tears, as I said, "Your sister is at our house."

She sat up in her seat and smiled. "Are we going home?"

"Of course!" I looked at her, her back rigid with excitement.

We rode back in silence, though anticipation was rushing through my veins. When we arrived home, Bernard swung the gate wide open with a huge smile. Micha ran ahead of me and I followed, pausing on the stairs while she bounded up onto the porch.

"Jessica!" she shouted in joy, squatting down and wrapping her arms around a tiny girl sitting on the porch, her legs stretched out in front of her.

"Michaëlle!" the little girl yelped back.

No words can explain the moment of their reunion. Trying to describe it here can hardly do it justice. I will never know how many years or months had passed since they had seen each other. And I will never know their full story.

In the corner sat their father. He smiled, but I'm not sure he could even begin to understand the miracle that had just happened.

I climbed the stairs and sat down on the porch next to Jessica. She backed away from me, fear in her eyes. Her white dress edged in blue lace was several sizes too small, and her toes hung off the ends of her dirty white sandals. I started talking to her quietly, telling her my name as tears squeezed out of her eyes.

Micha grabbed her younger sister's hand and spoke softly into her ear. "It's okay, Jessica. You are safe." Then she looked over at me and rubbed my arm, as if to say, *Go on.*

I couldn't. I looked at Micha, told her I'd be right back, then ran to the bathroom nearly blinded by tears. Before the door shut, I was on the floor sobbing. I thanked God out loud for allowing me to witness one of the most amazing moments in my entire life. Reunification. Love. Redemption. Jesus.

I knew I only had a few minutes to pull myself back together. I murmured a quick prayer of praise to the One who performs miracles. Then I dried my eyes, splashed water on my face, and went back to the porch.

There was a knock on the metal gate as the judge Bernard had called walked in. Within forty-five minutes, four-year-old Jessica's paperwork was finished and their father slipped out the door without saying good-bye. Maybe it was better that way.

I was excited and exhausted and talking to Bernard when I stopped midsentence, stricken. "Where is Jessica?" I didn't see her. My immediate thought was, *Great. I'm a mom of two for less than an hour and I've already lost one.* I looked out in the front yard, calling her name. Maybe she was hiding. I walked into the house.

"Jessica? Jessica?" I called, louder and slightly more panicked.

At the back of the house, a friend named Mr. George was standing on the porch. He had tears in his eyes. "She's right here," he called out, pointing down.

I walked closer, afraid of what I would see. There she was on the tiled back porch, a tiny little girl bent down, shoulders hunched, with a mop clutched in both hands. She was attempting to mop the porch.

I stepped out to the porch and looked down at her beautiful brown eyes, glazed over in fear. *Does she think I've brought her here to work for me?*

Slowly I pulled the mop out of her tiny hand. I couldn't believe that she even knew how to mop. I bent down, looked her straight in the eyes, and said, "Jessica. You don't have to do that here."

She backed away from me slowly, confused. A movement caught my eye; it was Micha peeking around the corner of the house. I waved her over and she came, tears welling up in her own eyes. I could see Micha's own painful memories on her face as she looked at Jessica and the mop. Micha walked slowly toward her sister, holding out her hand. Jessica looked up at me again, terrified, but this time I smiled back the tears and watched as she grabbed Micha's hand. They walked into the backyard together, holding hands, to play.

I crumbled to the floor of the back porch and rested my forehead on my hands. My heart felt as though it would implode with the cruelty of their situation. I throbbed with pain as I struggled to understand the confusion these two girls must be experiencing, about their worth, their identity, their rights as children, and now their freedom from being raised believing their only job is to serve others.

My mind flashed back to the feeding program at Bellevue Mountain. A group of restaveks had been trying to use a stick to scratch out their names in the dirt and laughing when they couldn't remember the right letters. My heart burned with a passion for them to learn not only how to spell their own names but also to attend school and feel as though they belonged there.

To build the new school on Bellevue Mountain for Micha, Jessica, and the other children, we were going to need more funding. As Jessica settled into our family, I began to pray and prepare for my second fund-raising trip back to the United States. My Haitian friend Tachi, almost like a sister to me, would be watching the girls.

I hated to leave since it was only a few weeks after Jessica's arrival, but I knew I had to do this for them. I had seen enough with my own eyes to know the need for education. I had enough stories of freedom through education that I was convinced it was the next step, and I had no doubt that God would provide for our school. What we needed was another miracle.

FIFTEEN

Be Bold

Never give up. And never, under any
circumstances, face the facts.
—Ruth Gordon

One week later on a Sunday afternoon, the cute guy who'd performed the skit in Gressier, Josh Anderson, was driving me to the Denver, Colorado, airport. He had become a friend, and had helped put together a fund-raiser for Respire Haiti in Fort Collins. We had left the church and were headed to the airport, but I was struggling, not knowing how much longer I could hold the tears back. I swallowed repeatedly, feeling as though a ton of tiny rocks were grating in my throat. As he drove, I could feel Josh's anxiety and knew he wanted to start a conversation. However, I was glad he kept quiet because I was pretty sure I wouldn't be able to open my mouth and say anything without breaking down into full-blown sobbing.

I wasn't crying because of Josh but because the fund-raiser had been less than successful.

My heart ached as I remembered how confident I'd felt in my prayers the week before. I just knew God would provide. But doubts had started creeping in, even before I left for my trip to the States. I'd started hearing whispers of criticism from other Americans serving in different cities in Haiti.

"Naïve girl."

"She will never make it in Haiti."

"This girl has no idea what she's getting herself into."

The comments echoed yet again in my mind as I rode in the car, and the tears won and started to trickle down my warm cheeks. Josh cleared his throat, breaking the silence and hesitantly asking, "Are you okay?"

"I'm sorry for being such a sensitive baby," I said in a hoarse voice. "I just thought this was going to look a little different."

"You don't need to apologize for crying," he said in a gentle voice.

I took a few more deep breaths before trying again. "I just felt *so* confident that the Lord was going to provide." Then I repeated the same story he'd already heard the night before, about how we had already started building the foundation for our six-classroom building at the school, and if I didn't return with more money, construction would stop. The tears were flowing fast now, down onto my shirt. I stared out the window, growing less embarrassed and more angry. I wanted to shake my fist at the heavens but refrained, not wanting Josh to think I was any crazier than he probably already thought.

Josh spoke up and began to softly remind me that God always provides for His plan, and it's always in His time and in His way. But it didn't help. Feeling more agitated than comforted by Josh's words, I turned and shot him a glare that I regretted as soon as I turned my head forward again.

The conversation lapsed back into awkward silence. I

replayed the previous night in my head. My sweet friends Rita and Brenda, Colorado women whom I had met in Haiti, had planned a wonderful evening for me. They had organized a home gathering with a group of people who wanted to hear about what God was doing in Gressier. I had felt relaxed and confident in the words the Lord gave me to share about Respire Haiti. *Why didn't anything happen, then?*

As I continued to battle with the Lord in my head, Josh's cell phone rang. Barely listening, all I heard was his brusque reply: "I'm sorry, but we're on the way to the airport. Her flight is at six o'clock tonight." He listened for a moment, then ended the call with, "Yeah, maybe next time," while his eyes stayed glued to the road.

I looked over at him, not that interested in the call. But he told me anyway, his eyes a little sad. "That was Mrs. Nancy Richardson, my boss's wife. She heard you speak last night and wanted us to have dinner with her and her husband, Curt, tonight."

Exhausted, I let the tears of anger, fear, and frustration pour out. I could faintly hear Josh apologizing and trying to comfort me, but the negative thoughts grew so strong I wanted to bang my head against the window and scream, *What am I doing? There are so many people depending on me in Gressier, yet I am going to disappoint them all.* This thought kept repeating, revolving around inside my head like the repetitive chorus of a song you can't seem to get rid of.

The car was silent again as I finally reached the end of my pity party and began to pray. I stopped thinking about myself and thought about Bellevue Mountain and the precious children there who needed a school, a safe and loving place to learn and to grow. I shuddered at how awful it would be to have to tell the forty construction workers that we could no longer continue building. I imagined how embarrassing it would be to tell Kyle, our builder who had just relocated from California to Haiti with a commitment to build our first six-classroom school building, that we did not have funding for his projects.

As the sorrow overwhelmed me, I took a deep breath, praying again. I thought about the freedom that Bellevue Mountain offered and the atmosphere of joy and peace. I closed my eyes, envisioning the school finished and full of children. I tried to release my feelings of guilt and shame at the failure of the fund-raiser, reminding myself that I was not solely responsible for supporting the construction workers, teachers, and students on Bellevue Mountain. *What a selfish thought that was.* I almost laughed at myself. Essentially I was thinking I was bigger than God. After all, He is the One who chose the workers, not me. He is the One who will provide for them, not me.

A peace came over me. I took another deep breath and released the anxiety and frustration. Then I looked over at Josh. "Thank you for all of your help and support, Josh."

"Hey, it's okay and . . ." He broke off when my phone rang.

I looked down at an unfamiliar number on the screen. "Uh, hello?" I said tentatively.

An auto-recorded voice came through. "This is American Airlines. Your six o'clock flight to Dallas/Fort Worth has been canceled. Your flight is rescheduled for tomorrow morning at 7:15 a.m." Goose bumps.

I dropped the phone and looked outside at the beautiful sky. Then I looked at Josh and practically shouted for him to pull over. My heart was beating so fast I couldn't organize my thoughts to get words out. Finally I gasped, "My flight is rescheduled for tomorrow morning!"

Josh let out a laugh. "Looks like we can go to dinner," he said as he immediately picked up the phone and called Mrs. Nancy back.

My mind raced as I began to recognize the illuminating signs of God's plan that was unfolding in front of our very eyes. Josh made a U-turn. I unbuckled my seat belt and crawled into the backseat to dig through my suitcase, hoping to find something semi-appropriate to wear for dinner. We stopped at a gas station so that I could change my clothes and then hurried off to meet Curt and Nancy Richardson for dinner.

As we pulled up to the restaurant, and before we stepped out of the car, Josh and I prayed. I tried to relax and not get my expectations up. I had already been let down and didn't want that to happen again.

"Even if it's just a few thousand dollars, we can continue working," I said to Josh as we walked inside.

"Let's see what God does," he said with a smile.

Curt and Nancy greeted us as we arrived at the table. I knew a little about them since Josh worked for their company, OtterBox, a manufacturer of protective cell phone cases. I felt extremely unprepared for this unanticipated meeting, but it didn't matter; they both stood up, hugged us, and made me feel very comfortable as they invited us to sit.

Mr. Curt began by asking Josh how his work was going. After a little small talk, he looked straight at me and exclaimed, "My wife was really encouraged last night by your story. She insisted I meet you."

I laughed nervously as the anxiety continued to rise up in the back of my throat.

Then he asked me questions about what God was doing in Gressier. I relaxed a bit and told him about our school, Micha, Jessica, and the restaveks. My words flowed and our conversation was lively, filled with lots of back-and-forth questions and responses. Then there was a pause.

Mr. Curt looked at me, his eyes intense, and asked a question I will never forget for the rest of my life. "If you could boldly ask for any amount of money for these children, how much would you ask for?"

My mind raced, and I began rambling something about the kids needing uniforms, books, and breakfasts.

"Boldly," he politely interrupted me.

A large amount popped into my head, but when I opened my mouth to say it, an amount exactly *double* the number came out. My eyes shot wide open in surprise when I realized what had happened. I panicked and wanted to reach out and physically grab the words and stuff them back inside. I sat there frozen, afraid that I had overstepped my bounds.

Mr. Curt looked at me and smiled. He reached around and pulled his checkbook out of his back pocket. I couldn't breathe as I watched him writing. My eyes began to blur as they filled with tears. He snapped the top back on his pen, then ripped out the check and closed the checkbook.

With a gentle, determined expression on his face, he reached out and handed me the check. Looking me straight in the eyes, he said in a calm voice, "I'm writing you a check for half of that, so you can continue to share your story."

I looked down at the check in my fingers, careful not to let my tears hit the fresh ink. I concentrated on breathing so as not to pass out. My blurry eyes could just barely make out the amount—it was more than enough to finish the school, buy the uniforms, cover the books and breakfasts, and pay the teachers for at least the first few months.

A picture of the kids in the feeding program scratching their names in the dirt rushed into my mind as I cried yet again. I felt God saying, *You are not doing this. I am. Let Me do it.*

I smiled back at Mr. Curt and Mrs. Nancy, as the words "thank you, thank you, thank you" kept pouring out of my mouth.

They both looked up with tears in their eyes and explained, almost in unison, "God has blessed us to bless others."

Images of Bellevue Mountain, the school, and the children flashed through my head again. *Trust Me,* I felt God saying, in those same words He had said to me from the very beginning, *This is My plan, not yours.* I pulled my Bible out of my purse and opened it, tucking the check in the center.

As I took a deep breath and tried to compose myself, I heard Mr. Curt say something to Josh. "So, I can see there might be something here." He pointed to Josh and to me.

Josh turned bright red and chuckled nervously.

"She was bold. Now it's your turn," he said to Josh.

Josh shyly nodded his head. Then Mr. Curt issued one of the most pivotal challenges in Josh's life. He said, "I want you to go to Haiti for a month and pursue what God is putting in front of you." And to make it possible, he offered to pay Josh's salary for the month so he could figure it out.

Like a deer caught in the headlights, his eyes wide, Josh shifted uncomfortably and nodded slowly, indicating he was willing to give it a shot. Embarrassed, he looked over at me and shrugged his shoulders, as if to tell me he had no idea that this would happen.

Like me, Josh had started a relationship with the Lord in college. He played basketball, baseball, and football and was dreaming about a master's degree in sports training. During his last semester, one of his best friends became a Christ follower. Josh noticed the difference in his friend's life, and before long, he began following Jesus too. Josh had been gradually learning to yield to God's voice and plan.

As quickly as the night began, it was over. We stood up and said good-bye. My heart was overflowing with the inspiration given to me by this couple I had only just met. I left that night completely encouraged, exhausted yet exhilarated. Josh and I had no idea, however, that we were about to embark on something even more life-changing, and challenging, than either of us could have ever imagined.

SIXTEEN

A Warning from
the First Lady

I believe that unarmed truth and unconditional
love will have the final word in reality.
This is why right, temporarily defeated,
is stronger than evil triumphant.
—Martin Luther King Jr.

Gabriel was gone, ripped out of my arms by a Haitian government agency after the orphanage sting operation, but
I had not forgotten him. It had been several weeks since the
sting, since he'd been taken—his nails clawing at my hands as
I reached out for him. They had locked him away in the back
of a white government sedan as I listened to his earsplitting
screams. That was also the last day I'd seen the orphanage and
Pastor Joe.

The Son of God Orphanage situation still sat in my emo-
tional in-box, marked "unresolved" in bright red ink. I had no
idea of Gabriel's whereabouts or even his safety. The only thing

keeping me going was Christ, my hope. I read the verses in the Bible that mention the angel Gabriel. My favorite was Luke 1:19: "I am Gabriel. I stand in the presence of God, and I have been sent to speak to you and to tell you this good news." I read that verse over and over. I was waiting, on Gabriel and the good news. Where was he? Micha missed him and asked about him often, and now Jessica had heard us talk about him so much she swore she knew him too. We prayed he was safe, healthy, loved, and secure. I knew—I believed—I would see him again. I continued to search for him and wanted him to know that I would never give up.

As bad as that was, what made me feel worse was the knowledge that even though Pastor Joe had been arrested months before, the orphanage had stayed open, stocked with dozens of other vulnerable children. Some of the older children, who knew where I lived, began running away to Gressier to tell me their horror stories about how they had not eaten for days. I could see by their emaciated bodies that they were telling the awful truth.

My heart grew increasingly heavy. My mind continued to flood with the thought that I could not give up on these children or on closing this corrupt and abusive orphanage.

My support team and I had been writing letters, staging meetings, and doing everything we could to spur the Haitian government to take action, but nothing seemed to budge. Finally some supporters in the United States had heard enough and decided to spring into action. Someone started an online petition at Change.org, and bloggers got on the bandwagon to spread the news and galvanize people to action:

Expose Human Trafficking at Son of God Orphanage in Haiti

We are petitioning CNN to bring their international media voice and passion for ending slavery into the Son of God Orphanage. Please urge CNN to expose the corruption within the Haitian government, and allow international organizations to secure the children from the child traffickers who are now controlling the orphanage.

The evidence in hand shows:

- Children have been and are currently being trafficked from the Son of God Orphanage. The evidence on human trafficking leads back to the Son of God Orphanage. The orphanage director was imprisoned in July as part of a police-led operation that resulted in his conviction of trafficking a child.
- Haitian investigators have told our team the evidence suggests trafficking, as well.
- Numerous photos show extreme physical abuse and neglect. U.S. and Haitian doctors have documented cases of severe abuse and neglect including burns and broken bones.
- As recently as October 10, 2011, American volunteers took children with late-stage starvation out of the orphanage and to local doctors. Without this intervention, the doctors

confirmed the children would have died of starvation.

This orphanage must be shut down. Other orphanages are ready and willing to take these children. Please urge CNN to cover this story and work to close this orphanage and re-locate the children immediately.

Sincerely,

[Your name][1]

The petition worked. Within twelve hours, more than ten thousand people signed. My phone started buzzing with calls from reporters and other media types, and I could tell something big was going to happen. Where I'd felt so stuck, defeated, and alone in my battle with the orphanage, now I felt as though a wall had been knocked down and everything was changing. I was ready for some good news, and I got some. My phone buzzed yet again, and this time I tried to process what I heard when I answered the phone, but all I could remember were the words *president's office*.

My heart sped up. Someone from the office of the president of Haiti was calling me. The man on the other end of the line asked me a few questions about the contents of the petition. With each question, I took a deep breath and tried to explain, to the best of my ability and knowledge of the facts, the truth about the selling of children at Son of God Orphanage.

The voice on the phone grew quiet, as if he was shocked and confused about how something like this could happen in Haiti. I was shocked, too, but *my* shock was because *he* was shocked this was happening in Haiti.

We talked more. I decided this was the perfect time for him to hear a little more about one of the biggest industries in the world. I explained the whole situation with Gabriel, and the dozens of other children who were missing from the orphanage. He thanked me for caring for the people of Haiti. Toward the end of the conversation, he asked if I could come in person to the presidential palace in Port-au-Prince to talk about the situation in the morning. *Tomorrow morning?* I was shocked, but I found my voice and told him I would be there.

I woke up early and got ready, putting on the one nice outfit I had brought to Haiti. But with the sweltering October heat and humidity, I was sweating immediately. Josh, who was on his one-month see-where-God-is-directing visit, drove me the two hours in a borrowed truck through the organized chaos of the capital until we reached the national palace compound in Port-au-Prince.

I stared up at the palace. Once white, gleaming, and beautiful like an ornate wedding cake, it was now crooked and crumbled, completely destroyed in the 2010 earthquake. We were directed to a huge tentlike structure that now housed the government of Haiti. While in line at security, I recognized a few familiar faces from the participants of the sting, realizing I was not the only one who had been summoned. After going through security, I had a moment to make a quick cell phone call. I called some of my advisors in Haiti, who urged me not to tell my story in front of anyone unless they were on the president's staff.

As Josh and I sat waiting for my appointment, I began to worry about what was happening behind the scenes. *Am I in danger? Is this some kind of set-up?* My chair was positioned next to a large green plant, and all I could see of the person sitting on the other side were two feet. I thought I might know her—oddly enough her shoes looked familiar—but I couldn't tell for sure. I decided to take a walk to the bathroom so I could get a better look at her face. I walked by and immediately recognized her from the numerous orphanage meetings; she had always resisted us pushing for action.

My heart started hammering. When I returned, the woman and I were both called in. She stood up and walked with a swagger straight to the office. I followed quickly, rehearsing what I was planning to say. Inside the office, the woman sat down in a chair facing the man behind the desk. I stood in the doorway, looked at the same man, and said in English, "I am willing to talk to you, but only if I am alone and no one else is in the room." Without waiting for a response, I wheeled around and went back to sit in the waiting room.

I texted the people involved, hoping for some sort of direction on how to handle this situation, when I received a text from an unknown phone number, reading, "The first lady knows you are here. She is coming to talk with you."

Wait, what? Who is this from, and how do they know who I am? Before I had any more time to think about it, or to talk to Josh, a tall woman in a smart business suit and pumps walked straight up to me and asked, "Are you Megan?"

I nodded. She pointed at me and told me to follow her. I stood up. Josh stood up, too, ready to go along with me. The lady pointed at him and then shook her finger in a quick, sharp, dismissive gesture, stating calmly, "She'll be right back." Josh got the message and sat back down. I shot him an anxious look, then followed her down the hall, my heart beating out of my chest.

She pointed to an office, where a poised and confident

woman was sitting. I squinted my eyes a bit, trying to remember where I knew her from, and then I realized *she* was the first lady of Haiti, Sophia Martelly. Her words were clear and measured as she explained that she and others were well aware of the orphanage, and now the petition, and they were working on the problem.

I reached into my reservoir of boldness once again and said a quick prayer. Then I looked at her and began the short monologue I had prepared.

"I love Haiti. I love the people here. I love what I do. But right now people are chomping at the bit to hear about the *bad* that is happening here. They are waiting on me to give them the dirty, ugly, evil details of what has happened. But I don't want to do that. I want Haiti to make the right choice in this. And I have to tell you, if this orphanage is not closed immediately, not only is it not the right choice, it will open the floodgates for bad media coverage. And we both know Haiti does not need more of that."

I paused and took a long breath, probably the first in my whole statement.

Mrs. Martelly nodded thoughtfully. "We will do this as fast as we can," she said, further explaining some of the details of the plan. She shook my hand, then told me to get myself out of there as fast as I could and warned me not to talk to anyone else about this. Her eyes stared into mine, and her mouth was set in a straight line.

At her words I felt threatened; confusion and fear rose up inside. *You mean I'm not safe here in the national palace of Haiti, with the first lady watching out for me?* I couldn't understand, but I believed her. I said a quick thank you, then grabbing Josh's hand on the way out, practically ran out of the building.

Later that day I got a call with more information about the timing of the orphanage closing and how it would all work. It sounded like a well-organized plan, and I prayed the boys and girls would be safe.

Our team had researched good orphanages for the children to relocate to after the closing, so I felt optimistic that this nightmare would soon end, at least for some children. The next day at midmorning I received phone calls alerting me that the orphanage had indeed been shut down. No longer would Son of God Orphanage use at-risk children to extort money and goods from well-meaning foreigners. I felt good about that. Relieved.

But there was some bad news as well. Instead of finding a hundred children, they found only about fifty. Stories began to trickle out about children running away, supposedly returning to extended family or finding other people to live with.

Although I received numerous requests for interviews, I was worried about what this kind of exposure might do to my organization, my life here in Gressier, and, most important, my girls, Micha and Jessica, who were staying with my friend Tachi. So I declined them all. Others did speak up and give interviews; ironically some of them were not even involved in the process. Others had actually perpetuated the abuse of these children by constantly bringing American churches and groups to come and "tour" the orphanage when it was opened.

After the orphanage closed, I began to receive e-mails from hundreds of churches who had partnered with other "bad" Haitian orphanages. These e-mails included disturbing reports of abuse, rape, and other horrors. The list of corrupt orphanages grew by the week as the light of truth found its way into Haiti's darkest and most desperate corners.

Son of God Orphanage had been a place filled with suffocating darkness, but the darkness did not win. The light won. Not only did the closing of Son of God Orphanage bring freedom; it brought to light what had long been hidden in the darkness: corruption, abuse, and evil. God was at work. In the following three months, more than twenty-five corrupt orphanages were closed.

My involvement, from my very first days in Haiti, caused me to rethink the common practice of American groups coming in and building, or supporting, orphanages without truly understanding the situation in Haiti. Especially since the plague of unemployment is so huge that it is believed 80 percent of all orphans end up in orphanages as a result of poverty. These "poverty orphans" are brought to orphanages mostly because their parents are unable to pay for food and school. Normally, American orphanages, or American-supported orphanages, pay for schooling for the children as well as for food, so to struggling parents these institutions look like the best and only option. However, with as many as 80 percent of orphans having a living parent, the rage to come to Haiti and build orphanages for these children seemed both broken and incongruous.

I realized that often what America thinks is the best for children is sometimes just a quick fix, a temporary Band-Aid that may ultimately exacerbate the situation. I knew there had to be a better way.

SEVENTEEN

School's In!

Education is the key to unlock the
golden door of freedom.
—George Washington Carver

I watched the children in their crisp new school uniforms line up in front of the dilapidated church. Two hundred students were about to make the walk from the old school we'd built, up to the beautiful new building on Bellevue Mountain. I held back tears as I remembered how we had prayed over and reclaimed the land used for voodoo ceremonies for many generations and battled to build the school from that very first moment when a voodoo priest had ordered us to stop putting in the fence around the property.

On impulse I looked down at my watch to see the time. As usual, we were running fashionably late. But my heart skipped a beat when the calendar date caught my eye. January 9, 2012. It was exactly one year to the day since I'd stepped off the plane in Port-au-Prince, wide-eyed, alone, terrified, and wondering if I'd made the biggest, scariest mistake of my life.

Now, lined up with the students in their light blue shirts and navy pants and skirts, the girls with their hair in pigtails tied with blue ribbons, I realized nothing had been a mistake at all. I looked at the kids' matching book sacks, heard their giggles, and felt excitement in the air. *These are children of the King*, I thought. I could almost hear God saying, with a big smile, "These are My children."

As we began to head uphill, Josh and I caught eyes briefly. I smiled shyly as I thought about the past few months, when he decided to quit his job at OtterBox and move full time to Haiti. After his boss had encouraged him to come spend a month here, we realized quickly that this was something we both wanted to continue.

Our dates consisted of getting gas together at the local gas station or going out to eat at Kayimit, the only restaurant in Gressier. There just are not many romantic spots for a couple to start a new relationship around Gressier; however, we knew when we started our relationship that dating in Haiti would be difficult. But we were both very committed to the fact that God had set this relationship up and He'd set it up *in Haiti*.

We began the uphill trek to Bellevue Mountain, the kids holding hands and marching two by two. As we walked, people along the way smiled and clapped. I could hardly contain my excitement, knowing the students had spent the first three months of the school year squished into a one-room church or under plastic tarps stretched overhead. Up on the mountain, things were going to be different.

After a fifteen-minute walk we arrived at the top. I could no longer hold back the tears. Just eight months earlier, I had known God wanted me to build a school. In obedience and faith, I'd built a tiny two-room school behind the church. *That is all I can do, God,* I remember thinking. *That is all the money I have. That is the biggest I can get.*

But I was wrong. And as I looked around the top of the mountain, my eyes widened in disbelief at the beautiful new school building with six classrooms.

Inside, the classrooms were light and airy, a soaring ceiling overhead with a white metal framework holding up the roof and letting light and air in through the eaves. The walls were a buttery yellow. And the smooth concrete floors were covered with neat wooden desks and benches.

Outside there was plenty of room to run, laugh, and play soccer on the grassy fields. And when it got hot, the tamarind tree offered a refuge of rest in its shade. At the edge of the mountaintop, we could see the Caribbean sparkling below, and behind were the deep green mountains looking over Bellevue.

I heard cheers of joy and excitement from the kids and the teachers, but before they scattered to their assigned classrooms, Mr. Gracia, the director of the primary grades, addressed the students. He began to talk about how big God is and how He made this happen. When he finished, Mr. Colin, another one of our directors, came up to pray over the students. He spread his arms wide, as if offering shelter, and thanked God for this beautiful new school on Bellevue Mountain, and the wonderful things ahead for the staff and the students. Many lifted their hands and voices to rejoice with him.

While Mr. Colin prayed, I looked around. Parts of the building weren't quite finished, and I saw plywood, building material scraps, and even a few nails lying around. My mama's heart lurched as I worried that the building wasn't quite ready for children yet. Then my spirit calmed as I chuckled and thought about the open manholes all over the city, the cars that drove so crazily our school crossing guard had almost been hit numerous times as he tried to do his job, and the other hazards the children faced every single day. I exhaled as the prayer finished, and I knew we were going to be okay.

The school staff looked at me to say something, but I was speechless, so I looked over and nodded at Kyle, our construction supervisor. Kyle had poured his heart and his soul into the construction of this first building. While he both taught American construction techniques and learned the Haitian culture of building, he never settled for anything below his high standard, yet he was patient. Kyle was a wizard at finding Haitian material and prided himself on using local labor in Gressier.

Kyle took my cue and walked up to say a few words. He moved slowly, and I could tell he was choked with emotion at the dream-become-reality, which he'd been a huge part of. He stood for a minute, and Bernard moved up to stand beside him and translate.

"This is *your* school," Kyle said to the children. "Your parents, your family, your community has built it for *you*. And we believe, we hope, that Respire Haiti Christian School will last for many years to come so that *your* kids can come here too." As he smiled and nodded his head, stepping back, the kids clapped and smiled too.

As Kyle and Bernard stepped away, I took their place. Seeing hundreds of children in uniforms was a beautiful sight. After all of the public expressions of thanks to God and to Respire and to me, I knew all I needed to say was one thing: "God is moving on Bellevue Mountain. He has built this school for you. It is God who has done all of this. He is bringing His light here."

The kids cheered, clapped, and then left in a big hurry to get into their classrooms for the very first time. As I walked under the walkway, peeking into classrooms, I looked at the scripture painted in beautiful script on the walls in each room. I saw the faces of the kids we'd been fighting to enroll in school, some for the first time in their lives. And trying to see through my clouded, tear-filled eyes, I saw story after story of redemption and beauty, sitting on new wooden benches on a smooth concrete floor.

I learned quickly that God's vision is bigger than mine, and I'm learning He knows the children of Gressier much better than I do. He is working out the details and He reminds me of this constantly.

One day I was picking up Michaëlle and Jessica from the new school when I ran into one of my neighbors who was picking up his three children. As we all walked home together, the kids ran ahead while we talked. This father began pouring out his heart, saying he'd had his children enrolled in another school before the earthquake. But when the earthquake struck, he lost his house and his job, and the school fees rose to the point where he had to take his kids out of school.

He looked at me with tears in his eyes and said, "Without you, without this school, my children would be at home. My children would not be learning. I thank God for you every day." He stopped to wipe his eyes. "Please know that we are with you. God bless you," he finished.

I looked at him and all I could murmur back was, "God bless you too."

He took his kids and went home. I stood in front of the open gate to our house, the girls already inside, and felt in shock. My mind whirled—not about how nice his comments were, or how sweet his words felt—but how big our God is. How big He is to orchestrate getting me to Gressier. How big He is to set up every step, polish every skill, forge every connection I needed to get me to the point of building a school for this man's three children to be part of. And how big He is to hold my hand for every step.

When most organizations in Haiti decide to build, the first thing they do with their land is build a tall cement block wall with barbed wire on top. God clearly told me from the beginning that He did not want Respire Haiti to do this. With both Haitians and Americans advising us to protect our land and building material with a reinforced cement wall, I politely disagreed. I knew it seemed naïve and maybe even foolish, but I had to stand firm on what God was telling me.

Shortly after this decision I began to see the fruits of trusting God. We added several more pieces of land on Bellevue Mountain that were adjacent to our first acre. Imagining the cost of tearing down a wall just to rebuild another one, I began to understand more just how wise God is and ultimately how imperative it is that I trust Him and His plan for Bellevue Mountain.

EIGHTEEN

The Binder from Hell

*No pen can give an adequate description of the
all-pervading corruption produced by slavery.*
—Harriet Ann Jacobs

I call it the binder from hell.

Pastor Charles was slowly flipping through the book as I
peeked over his shoulder. My heart sank deeper and deeper into
my stomach with each page. I knew the truth of this situation. I
knew the background of my children here, but for some reason,
seeing it on paper made it more real. The ink and paper made the
truth hurt more. It forced me to actually see and pay attention to
the real world I am living in.

Inside, we have created a record for every child in Respire
Haiti Christian School. When you open this book, it's like taking the skin off of every child in every classroom. Pastor really
understood my heart when I asked him to do this.

Pastor Charles has been my friend from the first few weeks
I moved to Gressier. Pastor is the husband of Madame Charles,
who served as the director of Respire Haiti's school. He is the

pastor of the church at the base of Bellevue Mountain, where the first tiny school was located.

He is also the person, with his wife, Madame, who prayed me into Haiti by meeting every Sunday morning for twelve years under the tamarind tree.

And, I didn't know this at first, but Pastor was a restavek. The stories of his childhood are haunting, but instead of feeling sorry for himself or becoming bitter and angry, Pastor has used his experiences as a restavek to fuel his passion for helping the children of his community have the opportunity to live in freedom and to be loved and valued.

He also grew up in a family that practiced voodoo. When he was thirteen years old, some Haitian missionaries came through the area and gave him a small Bible. He read it and turned his life over to Jesus. When he began to talk about his new experiences with the Lord, the community reaction was hostile, and his mother began to fear for his life, so she took him to Port-au-Prince to live with a relative, and from there it was all downhill. He bounced around from household to household, always beaten and treated worse than an animal. He remembers being bitten, starved, and forced to sleep in an outhouse.

He had no money, no family love or support, no education, and no hope for the future. At one point he went to school but was sent home one day for not having forty cents to pay his school fees. From that point he was forced to stay home and get up at three in the morning to work nonstop while he watched other children go to school. The only hope he had was the sense that God was with him. He finally was able to escape his life of abuse and slavery when a sponsor paid for him to finish school. He became a welder, married Madame, and began praying with her that they would always be in the center of God's will. "Whatever God says" is the guiding principle of his life.

When Pastor and Madame felt God calling them to Gressier, they started meeting up on Bellevue Mountain under the tamarind tree. Madame would spread a blanket under the tree. The first time it was just the two of them. Then they brought their children with them. Soon other believers joined them to pray. They became a large group, worshiping and walking around the top of the mountain, claiming it in the name of Jesus.

Because of the strong voodoo tradition in Gressier, especially on the mountain, there was much opposition. One particular voodoo priest had given a mandate that Pastor not be allowed to build a church, and they lost a piece of property they were planning to use for a church. But God finally answered their prayers and gave them a piece of land, where the church is located today. Pastor chose Titus 2:11 as the verse for their church: "For the grace of God has been revealed, bringing salvation to all people" (NLT). And "all people" includes children, especially restaveks.

Since Pastor was a restavek, he recognizes them. His heart is for truth and for freedom. He understands there is a deeper story behind every child at our school. So when you peek inside the classrooms at Respire, you will see beautiful children with clean uniforms, sitting up straight and smiling. They love school, love learning, and love to be here. It seems most students would stay at the school all day if they could. But once you pull back that thick and hardened skin of protection, open the binder, and see the lines and lines of *No mother. No father. Abandoned.* next to the names of our students, your blood boils. And when you read the word *restavek* again and again, you never will be the same. As I look at the binder, I often wonder what Michaëlle's entry would have looked like if Pastor had evaluated her situation before I became her mother.

When I look at the word *restavek*, I don't think about a definition or a statistic. I don't even associate it with particular individuals. I look at this word and think, *Darkness. Evil.* In the past some might have said the restavek system started out as a decent idea, almost functioning as a foster care system, where well-to-do families took in a child who was an orphan or at risk for some reason. But the system became corrupt, or maybe it was always corrupt. Children were expected to do more and more work, were treated poorly or abused, and were kept out of school.

In our school most of the children who are restaveks live with individuals who openly and religiously practice voodoo. Voodoo believes in possession, allowing a Iwa or spirit to come inside the individual's body, otherwise known as demonic possession. We have seen in our school, and outside of it, the harm and evil that voodoo can cause by this behavior. Oftentimes those who practice voodoo allow the darkness to completely take over their lives, and their houses are riddled with abuse, alcohol, and worse.

Many times we come in and clean the bloody wounds of children who have been beaten by a *rigwaz*. Rigwaz is a twisted leather strap used to herd animals, but it was also used to beat slaves. And although we have seen parents beat their children with sticks or rods in Gressier, more often in our area we see restaveks beaten using a rigwaz, and these brutal whips are sold openly in the Gressier marketplace.

A teacher once admitted that she had known Michaëlle before I had moved to Haiti. "Michaëlle was in a really miserable situation," the teacher told me. "I saw it. It was terrible. She was always working, always being treated terribly." I'd never heard this from her before, and I looked back at her in shock. I knew this teacher had lived close to where Micha lived in the tent on Bellevue Mountain, but I just assumed that because we hadn't spoken of it, she hadn't ever really noticed Micha's situation.

This unexpected conversation provoked a revelation for me—every person in Gressier knows what a restavek is, and they know which children are used as restaveks. But while most people in Gressier know it's wrong, hardly any people in Gressier know what to do. God spoke clearly to my heart in that next moment, saying, *Point them to Me. Point them to justice. Point them to freedom. Show them how to fight for these fatherless children.*

My mind raced as I quickly did the math. There are an estimated 300,000 to 500,000 restaveks in Haiti. My two girls were rescued. We have hundreds of restaveks at our school. We're working hard, but we're just one school in one community. We need help. We need the army of God to fight for freedom and be a voice for these children. This teacher reminded me how important it is for the entire community of Gressier, including teachers, not only to be aware of child trafficking, slavery, and abuse but also be shown how to take action, create change, and make freedom possible by treating children with dignity, justice, and love.

Our Respire staff visits and evaluates the homes of students and provides a good sense of the problems and challenges that face households in Gressier. We keep a close eye on the children, and the families and caregivers know we are watching them and keeping them accountable. We often make house calls to talk with our students' caregivers, parents, and families.

People often ask, "Why don't you just remove these children?" This was definitely my first thought when I moved to Haiti. Why not just take *all* of these kids out of these difficult, dark situations? Why not just walk over, grab the neglected child's hand, wag my finger in the adult's face, then let that sorry, pitiful caregiver watch the back of my head as I march away with the child in my arms, giving all the love and attention he or she deserves?

Some days this is all I want to do. I do want to swoop in and be the savior. Some days I don't want to have a two-hour conversation with an adult about discipline after I pull a stick out of his or her hands—a stick that was just used to beat and bruise one of our students from head to toe. Some days I don't want to have to visit the same house yet again, talking about how to discipline a child with love and respect when that child trusts no one and won't listen to anyone. Some days I don't want to clean the wounds of a child that was abused with a rigwaz.

It is so much harder to try to be the light of Jesus to the darkness than to be the white "savior" rescuing children. Sometimes it seems so much easier to take a child and put him or her in a place where he or she will get some good food and care.

But I have to be practical. I now understand that if I go and take a restavek out of a home, more than likely those people will just go and get another restavek and perpetuate the cycle. Suddenly I've just created more orphans, more homeless kids, and more restaveks. So I have to dismiss the lie that the only way to help is to spring into action and save these children by plucking them out as fast as I can.

The real truth, loud and clear, that I hear Jesus saying is this: be patient; be loving; be relational. Every day, and I mean *every day*, I have to pray against my flesh not to think of people who have a restavek as monsters. I want to curse and spit and yell at them for the way they treat these children—our students.

And then, again, I am reminded of the beauty and promise of education. The enemy oppresses people here by not allowing them the opportunity to understand discipline, good parenting, and most especially, children's rights. The myths that float around, mostly grounded in voodoo beliefs, can make you laugh, but when you realize people actually believe them, it makes you sick to your stomach.

Through all of this we know our school is not a normal school. It is a place where we reach the students, but we also care for and reach out to the parents, the families, and the caregivers. We have a unique opportunity to change the thought process of adults in Gressier. That is why Respire Haiti Christian School does what it does, and that's why we do it the way we do it.

One day I saw a boy outside the kindergarten room, standing with a group of parents waiting for the kindergartners to finish school. I approached him and bent down to ask his name. No response. I looked at him, his hands in his pockets, his eyes glued to the ground. This was a familiar scenario.

"What is your name?" I asked again. This time a mumble of something came out. I gently touched his chin to make his eyes meet mine, looked at him intently, and asked, "Are you in school?"

No response. I knew what that meant. But before I could probe any further, a man walked up and stood beside him. He told me the boy lived with him and was here to pick up a kindergartner who was a student at our school. I must have looked disgusted with the audacity of someone sending a restavek to our school to pick up a child. Just then, Pastor Charles walked up, saw my face, heard my tone of voice, and knew exactly what was happening. The three of us began to talk about the importance of all children going to school, how much our heavenly Father loves us, and how we are all children of God. Even though our enrollment was completely full, I could not stand the thought of this child coming to pick up another child from school every day for the next year. We told the boy, and the man he lives with, that his first day of school would be Monday. I saw a small grin on the boy's face, the first sign of emotion I'd noticed.

When Monday arrived, the boy was there bright and early. His name was Jean Louis, he was thirteen years old, and he had never been to school before. As I grabbed his hand to walk him to class, it was limp and his eyes stayed on the ground. I prayed silently as we walked, *Lord, show him who You are. Reveal Yourself to him. Give him courage, strength, and confidence in You. Help him to find his identity in You and not as a restavek.*

Toward the end of the day, his caregiver came to pick up the kindergartner and Jean Louis. We found Jean Louis sitting with four other children and their teacher, Monsieur Michel, going over the alphabet. Jean Louis sat in the front row grinning and talking with a smile. His life—and his freedom—are only beginning.

NINETEEN

Demons in the Trees

For he has rescued us from the
kingdom of darkness.
—Colossians 1:13 NLT

H ow many brothers and sisters do you have?" I asked Henry.
We were sitting together on a concrete bench at school. I had the binder from hell open on my lap, and I was asking this adorable boy a few routine questions about his family. He had this expression on his face, staring up at me, almost as if he was saying, *Do you really want to know?*

I tried again. "How many brothers and sisters do you have, Henry?"

"Two," he finally murmured, looking at the ground and kicking at some rocks.

"Two?" I asked, just to verify.

He looked back with wide eyes, then shook his head no. "I did have three, but one of them died."

He looked a little upset, and I didn't want to probe, so I stayed quiet. But he spoke again. "My uncle is a voodoo priest, and he took my little brother."

What?! A cold chill spiraled through my body, and I leaned down to listen. "How did you know, Henry?"

Then the story began to pour out of him. He'd overheard the conversation between the voodoo priest uncle and his parents, who were arguing and wanted to keep the little brother. He heard his uncle shouting that the parents owed him money and he was going to take the child as payment. So he did.

After the uncle took Henry's little brother, he never saw him again, and he overheard his parents grieving about how the priest had killed him.

A few weeks later the voodoo priest came back again, this time for Henry. He told me how he remembered his uncle demanding that his mother give him up, just as she had with her younger son. His mother began to cry, and Henry became frightened and ran outside. He went behind the house and squatted down to pray, squeezing his eyes closed.

"Jesus, save me," he called out. "Please help me and keep me safe," he begged out loud.

After a few minutes Henry opened his eyes, and it took a moment for his vision to clear. Confused, he realized he was no longer at the back of his house, and he believed that he somehow had been supernaturally whisked away from that place of danger.

"Jesus saved me," Henry said to me. I can still hear his earnest voice saying those three words. They're engraved on my soul.

I sat there in near disbelief. I'm sure my jaw dropped, and Henry could see the shock on my face, but he didn't flinch, not one bit. I didn't know what to say, so I tried to think of something light. I blurted out, "So you love Jesus?"

Henry looked at me with a twinkle in his eye and said, "Of course. He saved my life."

I felt as if the wind had been knocked out of me as I sort of nodded my head and managed to say, "Henry, you can go back to class now." Then my head and my heart started to fight. *Should I believe him? Should I not believe him?* I heard his words over and over in my head and wrestled with whether it could possibly be true that Henry had prayed and immediately Jesus had physically transported him from a very evil and life-threatening situation to a place of safety. And now here he was, enrolled at our school.

I finally surrendered to the fact that this was Henry's story. Who am I to judge whether it is true or not? But after that moment I prayed to keep an open mind and heart about what the children say. For starters, they often talk about having terrible nightmares—being pulled under the sea, hearing awful sounds, or seeing terrible things. One thirteen-year-old student told me he didn't want to go home for Christmas break because there was a voodoo altar in his front yard and he was tired of seeing "demons jumping out of trees."

My heart aches at hearing stories about parents paying voodoo priests out of fear, instead of paying for a child's education. Or a child dying from malnutrition because the family owed the "spirits" too much so they continued to offer their only food to the cross in the middle of their yard. (In Haiti crosses are often related more to voodoo than to Christianity.)

There are times we see white powder sprinkled on the mountain or on the roads in the shape of circles or other symbols, most times with broken glass, candles, or even blood or bits of bone left behind. We've seen blood sacrifices on Bellevue Mountain involving chickens, cows, and horses. There are whispered stories about the sacrifice of children, but there are plenty of people in the global community and Haiti who deny these stories and defend voodoo as a longtime cultural practice that we should not interfere with.

While I thought I understood the battle for Bellevue Mountain, the longer I am here, the more I know I don't even know the half of it. But the fear that voodoo priests and others in the community tried to instill in me by urging me to get away from Bellevue Mountain only made my desire to be in God's will that much stronger.

My prayer from the very beginning has always been this: *Lord, if You would like us to have this land, make it easy and make it simple.* Without fail God has made it simple. He has always provided the money, and the paperwork has been easy and smooth, which is a feat in Haiti. We prayed and prayed over the purchases of our second, third, fourth, and fifth pieces of land. God provided and the Respire Haiti Christian School campus grew by four more classrooms protected by our staff, by the community, and by God's angels.

After we'd purchased five pieces of land, totaling about four acres, I sat on a sixth piece of land nearby. I began praying for the school, the staff, and the students. Then a thought crossed my mind. *Pray for this land.* I laughed out loud. *I have no idea what to do with this piece of land. We have everything we need.*

But I felt that nudge and I closed my eyes and said a quick prayer. *Lord, if You want us to have this land, then make it simple and make it clear.*

My eyes snapped open at the ring of my cell phone. I looked down at the screen and saw Pastor Charles's name. I picked it up and punched the Talk button. "Hello?"

"Megan, you know the land that touches our soccer field and is close to the Caribbean?" Pastor said.

"Yes. I'm sitting on it now," I said.

"Great." Pastor chuckled. "The owner just asked if we want to buy it."

God's direction was crystal clear, so clear it shocked me. "I'll think about it," I responded hastily, and hung up.

I felt that the Lord wanted us to move forward, so I began telling the staff and interns about the call and everyone was excited. We decided to pray on this piece of land, but little did we know that we were about to step into battle.

Almost every evening for three months, we trekked up to Bellevue Mountain to pray. On one of the first nights, I felt a sense of evil as we approached. Near the area where we usually prayed and worshiped, I spotted a figure moving toward me quickly. Within a few moments we were facing off. It was a man, towering above me, wearing a gold robe that hung down from his long arms. He acted as though he had something to say, so I waited for him to speak first. My team waited a good distance behind.

The man stepped closer. When he moved, a flashlight from someone behind reflected off a large machete he held in his left hand, near his leg.

I felt an overwhelming sense of darkness and evil emanating from him. I looked up into his eyes, and they were deep pools of endless black. I gasped and took a small step back, feeling as though something was grabbing me tightly. I prayed under my breath for protection and courage.

He looked down at me. "You have interrupted, and you need to get off this land immediately."

My blood began boiling, and I thought of all sorts of defensive and combative things to say, but I closed my mouth. I looked back up, avoided his eyes, and nodded. As I turned around and motioned for everyone to follow, my head spun. *What should I have done? Maybe I should have told him to get off of this land. It's our land. It's God's land!*

But, instead, we walked back over to our soccer field, adjacent to this new piece of land, and began to pray, facing our new friend in the gold robe. One of our sweet, young interns asked, "What should we do?" As her voice echoed in my heart, I took a deep breath and remembered how many people I was responsible for. *God, thank You for keeping me calm and levelheaded. Show us what to do and how to pray.*

During this period of praying on the mountain, this type of confrontation became the norm. Many times we walked up on people performing voodoo rituals on the land, or voodoo priests approached us as we worshiped. Cars full of men would drive onto the property, waiting for us to finish worshiping so they could use the land. Almost every night was a battle of who would get there first or stay the longest.

Although our prayer team was always the same, the voodoo priests constantly changed. It seemed as if dozens upon dozens of people intentionally used this part of Bellevue Mountain to perform voodoo rituals. One evening after finally getting the courage to ask why the voodoo priests wanted to come to the mountain, one of them replied firmly, "Didn't Jesus go to the mountain to pray?" His slithery voice made the hair stand on my arms. I thought about how dark and convoluted he had made the precious words of Jesus as He spoke of retreating to the mountains to pray.

Nearly every morning we'd see evidence of large ceremonies in the grass or on the rocks on Bellevue Mountain. We would see the residue of blood, glass, and powder. The battle for this piece of land was the hardest out of any of the six pieces we purchased, mainly because it was the last piece of land on top of Bellevue Mountain. It was also the largest piece, and it over-looked the beautiful, blue Caribbean water.

After two months of intense prayer, the money was provided, and we purchased this piece of land, but we didn't stop praying. By God's grace, we have been able to complete the construction of our medical and dental clinic, which is located on a part of this property. The clinic will serve our students, their families, and the community as well. The site is beautiful; visiting dentists and doctors have a 180-degree view of the Caribbean from the front door of their guest room at the back of the clinic.

The clinic covers about half of the land, which seemed so attractive to the voodoo priests for their ceremonies. And the other half? I'm dreaming about building a church there.

TWENTY

Josh Has Something to Say

When you give yourself, you
receive more than you give.
—Antoine de Saint-Exupéry

I hiked quickly up Bellevue Mountain, knowing that I was supposed to lead morning prayer. I was running late, but still I wondered why everyone had gone up without me. I picked up the pace and met up with one of my best friends who had been serving with us at Respire Haiti.

Jessi White is one of the most joyful and hilarious people in my life. Her southern drawl is one of a kind, and her support and encouragement mean the world to me. As we walked together, my step got lighter, and I stopped wondering where everyone was.

When we arrived, Jessi laughed and said, "It isn't good for you to be so late for prayer when you're leading it. You better hurry!" I scurried through the gate in front of her and walked as fast as I could to the flagpole.

The kids were gathered as usual, standing in straight lines, dressed in their crisp navy and light-blue uniforms, big smiles on their faces, around the flagpole, where the bright-red and royal blue Haitian flag flew. In the center of the flag is the Haitian coat of arms, a palm tree on a green hill. Under the hill are flags, cannons, and other weapons, and the motto *L'Union Fait La Force*, or "Unity through strength."

After they line up, the kids salute the flag, sing the Haitian national anthem, and then pray together as one of the administrators, usually Pastor Colin, leads through a megaphone. Today I would be praying, so I headed to the front.

Pastor Colin walked up before me, held the megaphone, and began praying. In Haiti it's not unusual to have a prayer before the prayer. Then he led the children in singing "How Great Thou Art." I love hearing them sing with all of their hearts, knowing the depth and truth of those words. As they came to the end of the song, I inched forward, knowing I was next. Pastor Colin looked my way and nodded. I stepped in front of the whole school, the children with their teachers, and reached for the megaphone.

But then Pastor Colin pulled the megaphone back toward himself and lifted it up to his mouth again. I was so confused that it didn't quite register in my brain what he was saying—something like, "Josh has something he wants to say."

In complete shock I heard a huge uproar from the kids and a tremendous shout. It was a chorus of hundreds of children's voices of all ages yelling, "Weel. You. Maywee. Mee?"

My eyes widened and filled with tears as I looked out at the faces of these precious children who were smiling with glee. In the front row was a group of first graders, holding up a big painted sign that said "Will you marry me?" I noticed the kids were smiling, laughing, and focusing on something behind me. I turned around, and there was Josh on one knee with a ring in his hand!

"Yes," I squeaked out, barely. Micha and Jessica ran up and hugged me, and suddenly we were surrounded by friends and family who wanted to share in the moment.

For the rest of the week, I must have heard the proposal repeated hundreds of times. Every time I turned around, "Weel you mawry mee?" popped out of a child's mouth in the cutest Haitian accent. On top of that, Micha and Jessica began asking if they could call Josh "Dad."

When the excitement of the student-assisted proposal had died down a bit, we realized we needed to start actually planning a wedding. I talked things over with Jessi, so grateful that God had orchestrated her schedule so she could be in Haiti when I got engaged and could help me plan my wedding. She suggested Josh and I spend a day at the beach and make our plans while she watched the kids.

As Josh and I walked down the coast, our toes dipping in and out of the warm, turquoise waters, we decided we wanted to heed the advice of some of our best friends: "Short engagement, long honeymoon." We chose January 22, 2013, to be our wedding date, which would give us about two months. Divinely, it was also the same date that Josh had become a Christian four years earlier. It was a quick timeline, but we thought if we invited people right away it just might work.

As soon as we got back to Gressier, we sent e-mails out to friends and family with the wedding date. After a few quick notes of congratulations, I received an e-mail from my mom. "You *do* realize January 22 is a Tuesday, right?" I grabbed a calendar. *Argh. She's right! How did that happen?*

I panicked, made a quick call to Josh, and ended up laughing with him on the phone about how horrible we are with dates. Then we decided, "You know what? Tuesday, January 22, is going to be perfect." So we kept the date.

As RSVPs began to arrive over the next few weeks, one stood out—from Curt and Nancy Richardson, the wonderful couple who had supported Respire from the very beginning with the "be bold" challenge. Nancy wrote that they could not come, as years ago they were married on January 22 and would be celebrating their anniversary the same day as our wedding in Haiti. I smiled at the irony of this.

Christmas and New Year's kept us all busy and I didn't get much wedding planning done, so Jessi stepped in and did most of the work in January in the three weeks leading up to the wedding. When my mom and uncle arrived, we picked them up at the airport. It was their first time to Haiti, so we carefully drove through the traffic and spectacle of Port-au-Prince explaining the oddities of this chaotic yet beautiful place. The moment became surreal. I had never in my wildest dreams imagined getting married on a mountaintop in Haiti.

January 22, 2013, was a beautiful day, and I married my best friend, Josh Anderson, on Bellevue Mountain under a bright blue sky. I looked out to see hundreds of children with their school uniforms on, smiling and giggling as we said our vows. I chuckled as a lady I had never seen before poked her head above the crowd to sell bread in a box to the more than six hundred people and a few chickens lining the grassy area on Bellevue Mountain. Smiles from our teachers and friends, Haitian and American, lit up the whole crowd.

I looked back at Josh, so handsome in his brown suit, and

wondered, *Who is this man, who would come to live in Haiti with me? And with Micha and Jessica?*

As I held my uncle T-tone's arm tightly before we headed down the aisle, I closed my eyes, drinking in the moment and thanking the Lord for Josh. God had brought us together, and now I had someone who would always be there to love me, help me, encourage me, and make me smile.

After celebrating with family and friends, Josh and I flew to another Caribbean island for a week's honeymoon. When we returned to Haiti in early February, the first of many new issues greeted us, but this time as a couple.

A Respire student named Saintil was worried about his sister, Johanne, who hadn't returned to school after the holidays. He was only nine years old, so his answers to my questions didn't always make sense. But I could feel his deep concern for her and I took it seriously.

Not only were Saintil and his sister our students, but they were true orphans with no father or mother. After arriving in Gressier only six months earlier, we had enrolled them in school for the first time ever and had been monitoring them closely. Saintil said his sister was staying with someone in a distant city, but he didn't have the address. He did say he had been there once and insisted he could find it again.

I saw the fear in his eyes and knew we had no choice. To ease his mind and ours, we would have to drive and try to find this place where she was staying to make sure she was okay. It was a needle-in-a-haystack mission, but as I looked down again at sweet Saintil, I could feel the worry radiating from him.

Within a few minutes Josh and I jumped in the car with Saintil. Jessi came with us, and so did Wadley, a trusted staff member from the school, whom I knew would help with anything that might come our way. We started off toward the part of Haiti where we thought she was located. Driving through the city, we listened to Will Reagan sing about taking back what the enemy had stolen.[1] I looked over at Josh, on yet another adventure with me. Would this one be a wild goose-chase? We'd already been on a few of those together.

Josh had sensed my gaze, looked over at me, and smiled. "I feel like we're literally driving into the pits of hell," he joked. He could make me smile in almost any circumstance, and I loved that about him.

As we got closer to the town, we began asking Saintil questions about which roads to take. Josh followed the direction of Saintil's tiny finger as it pointed right, then left, showing where to turn. We were all nervous, wondering if this child who had been to this location only once, would be able to successfully lead us there. Haiti is not an easy place to navigate when you get off the main highway and go back into the winding dirt roads without signposts, and no help from maps or GPS.

We began to drive up and down back roads, making wrong turns and having to backtrack through clusters of shacks and tent cities. A few times we were forced to stop and ask for directions, and after several stops it became clear that we were lost, and our quest seemed almost hopeless. Josh and I looked at each other in frustration, wanting to give up, but I felt the Holy Spirit tug at our hearts, saying, *Continue on.*

The road started to become smaller and smaller until it was just a path, and we had to stop the car and walk if we wanted to continue. I really couldn't make out much of an opening and assumed we were at another dead end and would need to turn around, but then Saintil seemed to recognize the area. He swung open the back door of the car and got out. I prayed, then hopped out after him. He started walking fast, and we hurried to keep up.

There were dozens of tin shacks packed together, and we followed Saintil on the rough path through rusty gates. I kept asking the Lord to go before us and I felt certain He would lead us to the right place. "Divine guidance," I whispered out loud as we followed Saintil, still marching ahead. I had no idea how he could remember the way.

After a few more minutes of walking up a mountain and weaving in and out of yards, Saintil slowed, grabbed at my hand, and tugged me forward. I looked where he was looking and saw a gate made of bent scrap metal held together by patchwork wire. Saintil pushed forward, looked back at me with burning eyes, and pulled the gate open.

I stepped inside, and before I could take a breath, I saw her. Johanne stepped forward out of the darkness. Our eyes met, and she stopped in her tracks, tilting her head as she gazed at me. The next second, she launched herself at me, full speed, and hugged me, squeezing with all of her strength. I hugged her frail body and kissed her forehead.

"Where have you been?" I exclaimed. "Everyone is asking about you! Why haven't you been at school?" She looked up and hugged me even tighter, a smile growing on her lips.

Then I looked around. Slowly the surroundings came into focus, and I stared in horror at the voodoo paraphernalia all around us. The burnt wooden crosses, oily animal skulls, and powdery altar seemed to move inward and close in on me, and

I realized we had walked straight into a voodoo temple. The Haitians call it *Kay Djab*, the house of the devil.

Johanne was living inside. *What in the world is she doing here?* I wondered. I soon would find out.

TWENTY-ONE

The House of the Devil

When I am afraid, I put my trust in you.
—Psalm 56:3 ESV

Where are you staying? And with whom?" I asked Johanne. "My mother's ex-boyfriend," she said, her face becoming an expressionless mask. "He isn't here right now."

I knew her mother had died many years earlier, so I still wasn't sure who had brought her to this place, or why. I heard a noise from behind Johanne and saw curious faces peering at us from windows and doorways.

"Let's take a walk," I said, and took Johanne by the hand. She grasped my hand tight, and we'd barely made it out the front gate when she pulled me close and whispered in my ear.

"Please take me with you." Her voice was urgent.

"Are you okay?" I asked quietly, squeezing her hand with a gentle touch.

"I don't want to stay here. But I don't want to go back to the people in Gressier either. They beat me," she said, her voice dropping off so I could barely hear. She looked down and away. She was twelve years old, about to become a young woman, but she was the size of my nine-year-old Micha. I felt my face get hot in anger as I thought about all the times I'd visited her home in Gressier, keeping an eye on her and Saintil and trying to work with her older brother with whom she was living. Then as the flush of anger faded away, my heart broke for her.

We turned around and walked back to the voodoo temple. Inside, Wadley and I took turns, asking the adults hanging around the temple where we could find the man who had brought Johanne to this place. A lady in her midforties rolled her eyes in disgust and refused to answer. We kept asking, and she finally barked out, "I'm not the one responsible for her. I can't say anything."

Next, we asked if she had a number so we could try to give him a call. "He has no phone. It's lost," she snapped. "He's gone, and I don't know when he'll be back."

"Can we wait here for him?"

She shrugged her shoulders and turned her back on us.

We decided to wait outside the gate, away from the voodoo paraphernalia, the watching eyes, and the dark and heavy atmosphere of the place. I asked Wadley what he thought. He responded firmly and with confidence, "This is serious. I think God wants us to take her."

I leaned in. *Are You sure, Lord?* I asked. My chest tightened, wondering how we could make it happen. We were clearly outnumbered, and I didn't want to break the law and be accused of taking Johanne from a place where she was living.

But Wadley continued. "We will leave with her today. God will make it happen." I agreed, and we began to pray for the man to arrive soon.

Seconds later I heard a rustling, and someone shouted for

us. We quickly returned to the wire gate, and up stepped the man who had been Johanne's deceased mother's ex-boyfriend. He motioned us in, and the feelings of oppression and evil were even stronger than before. The man looked up and welcomed us to his home. *"Bonswa,"* he said with a slight grin, waving me to a chair.

His grin slowly turned into a crooked smirk, and I felt sickened. When I introduced myself and everyone else, I immediately sensed his resistance to us. *He is never going to let Johanne go,* I thought. When I explained that we missed Johanne at school, his smirk grew deeper, and he seemed to think our caring about her was something funny. His face took on an arrogant, mocking expression, while Johanne stood behind him, waiting.

After a small prayer asking God to show me what to do, I opened my mouth with no real plan, and the Holy Spirit took over. I'd had this experience a few times before, with the Lord showing His power as my Creole becomes impeccable and I use words and Haitian proverbs I've never even heard before.

Words poured out of my mouth as I began explaining the importance of Johanne's presence at school and how we were blessed to have a place for her to live. It seemed to take ages for me to explain why we wanted her to come with us, and I don't remember much else, except praying through it all and hearing Jessi, Josh, and Wadley's whispered prayers as they stood behind my chair.

When I finished, the man began saying nonsensical things, such as how he needed to "prepare her" and how she couldn't leave until he'd made the "preparations." This made me only angrier. *A voodoo priest talking about preparations on a young girl? Not on my watch.*

Wadley jumped in, a concerned look on his face, and said boldly, "We have everything she needs. No preparations are necessary."

The man started to shake his head, a regretful sigh escaping his lips as if he were preparing us for a "no."

"I cannot allow her to come with you without talking to her older stepbrother," he said. This was the same person who'd been beating her in Gressier. At this point the chances of this man allowing Johanne to come with us were slim. But somehow I began to feel more confident. I turned around to look at my husband, my dear friend Jessi, and Wadley, and suddenly I felt as if God's armies of angels were encamped around us. The atmosphere grew a little lighter and brighter, as Jessi winked and smiled, Josh's face betrayed the righteous anger that the Lord had given him, and Wadley stood confidently waiting for God to win.

Just then, the man glared down at Johanne and said, "Well, what do you want to do?" His tone was threatening and dripped with sarcasm.

She looked at the ground and said quietly, "Go with them."

"What do you think of that?" the man asked his girlfriend.

"I don't care," she answered in a nonchalant voice, not even bothering to look up.

He shrugged, looking at Wadley. "I'll tell her older stepbrother where she went." Then he growled at Johanne, "Get your bags."

She disappeared somewhere inside and came out within seconds wearing a shirt three sizes too small and pants three sizes too big, and she was carrying a book sack she had received at Respire's school that contained only her uniform. Johanne turned around and looked at the other children accumulated there, watching. No good-byes, no hugs, no anything from anybody, including the man. Then she turned around with a small smile and marched right out of the gate.

We followed as fast as we could and raced to the car, wanting to be out of there. Johanne held my hand as we walked, squeezing it as hard as she could. We were quiet, incredibly overwhelmed with emotion. Inside the car we sat silent for a moment, then laughed, cried, and talked about how God is all-powerful, and how He is a warrior for His children.

Saintil sat stone-faced as we began to drive. "Are you okay?" I asked.

He nodded yes.

"Are you happy?" I asked.

Another nod.

"Do you see what you did?" I asked him softly. "Do you see what God used you to do? You fought for your sister. You led us here!" My voice rose in excitement. I was so proud of him. "We couldn't have done this without you. It's okay to cry. They are tears of joy, and God wants us to be joyful. We are together now, and Jesus was with us the whole time."

As Saintil listened to my words, his eyes began to fill with tears and he wiped them away with the back of his hands. Then the floodgates opened. I held him and said, "It's okay. We know you missed Johanne and God has given you such great love for your sister."

Saintil continued to bawl in Jessi's lap and clung to his sister's hand all the way home.

Johanne came home with us that night, and we were exhausted, still in shock from the confrontation with that evil, sarcastic, mocking man who had some sort of dark plan for her.

But God had other plans, and trying to comprehend what God had just done blew my mind. God fights for the fatherless, because the battle is so real.

We had been listening to that song about plundering the pits of hell, and we had literally, ironically, divinely rescued Johanne from the devil's house. We had walked into his house and snatched Johanne from his grasp in the name of Jesus. God is the most amazing warrior, and the most courageous, strong, and beautiful example of a father. Johanne and I are both fatherless, and I love that God is Johanne's Father, and He is mine too. And because of Him, we won. We were victorious.

This is the gospel. One person at a time. One child at a time. Progress might seem small and slow at times, and it might seem impossible to ever really make a difference, but it is moments like this when we are reminded God is at work.

We settled back into life in Gressier, and Johanne stayed with us as she recovered. Not long after she was back, she came home from school one day in a panic. "My older stepbrother is in trouble, so he took Saintil!" she said. I asked where her older brother was, but she didn't seem to know. I was worried and made a few phone calls that all led to nothing. Feeling as if there was nothing we could do, I began to pray and beg God to bring Saintil home. Days turned into weeks. Five weeks had passed when one evening, as we were eating dinner, a knock on the metal gate echoed across the front yard.

"Who is it?" Josh called out.

No answer.

"Who is it?" I repeated, in Creole.

A small voice, barely audible, responded on the other side. Someone downstairs opened the gate, and there stood Saintil. This little nine-year-old boy had been missing from Respire Haiti Christian School for more than a month. He limped in, exhausted, looking completely worn-out.

I flew down the stairs and bombarded him with big hugs, kisses, and smiles. The corners of his mouth lifted, just barely. It was clear that something was different in this boy who was usually so joyful and full of life.

The first question out of his mouth, after he came in and sat down, was, "Where is Johanne?" We sent someone to go get her immediately. Saintil couldn't seem to explain where he'd been or answer our questions in a straightforward manner. Things were not adding up, and we could tell he was hesitant to give us all the facts.

Saintil looked frail, as if he was starving, but he wouldn't eat anything I offered him. As I looked with a hurting heart at his sunken eyes and exhausted body, some of his answers finally started to connect and make some sort of sense. He had arrived on foot from Jacmel, a town almost three hours away *by car.* He'd left early in the morning the day before and walked over numerous mountains and through valleys to Gressier, walking and walking and walking to return to his sister.

As we listened, tears filled our eyes. He had walked for two days on foot, with no food, to get here. That's how badly he wanted to see his sister, Johanne. Besides his abusive older stepbrother, Saintil's sister is his only family, and he knew if he came to our house, he would find Johanne. My mind spun with the beauty and sadness of his story.

When Johanne heard Saintil was at the house, she sprinted toward her brother and slammed into him, nearly knocking down his emaciated body as she embraced him with joy. She looked up at us wide-eyed, her eyes screaming out what her heart wanted to say: *He can't go back there.*

"Saintil needs to go back to school," she said in a firm voice. "Everyone misses him."

She chattered to her brother, telling him how she had done well in school this last trimester and that if he had been there for testing, he would have passed too. (Both Johanne and Saintil were in a class specially designed for children who had never been to school before; the program took them through first and second grades in one year.)

Then Johanne slid a bracelet off her wrist and put it on Saintil. "Team Jesus," the bracelet read. She hugged him and smiled again, bigger than before.

"No one wants us to go to school," she said to us in a strong, clear voice. "Saintil can't go back to Jacmel or they will never let him go to school."

As Saintil's head hit the pillow that night, I prayed over him. I thought about the miles his feet had walked, the sights his eyes had seen, and the hunger, fatigue, and fear he had suffered on his long journey.

It still wasn't clear exactly where he had been or how he came to leave in the first place. But as he drifted down into peaceful sleep, knowing he was close by his sister and in the arms of people who loved him, I couldn't help but pray that Saintil felt at home. Not only because he was in our home, with Josh, Micha, Jessica, Johanne, and me, but because he was sleeping in the sweet arms of Jesus.

TWENTY-TWO

The Woman at the Gate

Thank God for the battle verses in the Bible. We
go into the unknown every day of our lives.
—Amy Carmichael

One beautiful, warm evening the night guard called out to
me as soon as he arrived. "Megan? Megan!" There was a
note of distress in his voice, so I crept down the stairs and met
him on the front porch.

"There is someone sitting outside the gate," he said, pointing into the dark. I followed him across the yard and waited as
he rolled the heavy metal gate back a few inches so I could peek
outside. *It's her! The woman Jessi and I saw.*

Earlier that day Jessi and I had been walking back home from
Bellevue Mountain, chattering and happy. When we turned the last
corner before our home, I saw someone sitting outside near our house
on some rocks by the side of the road. The figure looked odd—sort
of slumped over—but we could tell it was a young woman.

I tugged on Jessi's arm and pointed, trying not to make any noise until we knew if she was sleeping, or ill, or something else. But Jessi had a different plan. She yelled out to the woman, "Hey! Are you okay?"

The motionless figure began to move, slowly raising her head from her lap. She looked straight at us and smiled a creepy smile that gave you no choice but to look away. The woman said nothing, just stared as if she were looking right through us. I was chilled to the bone in the midst of the Caribbean heat, a feeling I had become all too familiar with.

She looked frail but otherwise okay, despite the faraway look in her eyes, so Jessi and I continued through the gate and into the front yard. I looked over at my friend and without saying a word, we both understood the darkness that was crouched outside on the rocks.

As I walked into the yard, my spirit felt unsettled and I began to pace around the house and pray and sing to the Lord. As I worshiped in every single room of the house, Micha joined in with me, following behind and singing in her young, soothing voice. As I looked down and smiled at her sweet, calm spirit, I felt relieved. I was upstairs by now and I glanced out the window and over the balcony railing toward the pile of rocks where the woman had been perched. No one was there. I could feel the relief wash over my body.

After that, I went on with my afternoon, spending time with the kids, making sure homework and chores were getting done, and sitting down to dinner with the whole family. After we ate dinner we played, took baths, had story time and prayers, and Josh and I put the kids to bed.

So when the night guard called, the routines of the day had

pushed the strange woman on the rocks to the back of my mind. But now, as I craned my head around and saw her again, those dark feelings came back. She was wearing the same clothes and still sitting in that odd slumped position while staring off into the distance.

I exited the gate, and as I began walking toward her, I prayed fervently. *God, tell me what to do.* I approached, slow and cautious, and called out to her quietly. She sat up a little straighter, slowly turned her head toward me, and looked vacantly into my eyes.

Her gaze made me gasp, and I felt as though the wind had been knocked out of me. I wanted to turn around and run back inside to warmth, light, and safety, but instead I forced myself to step closer. "What is your name?" I heard her mumble something, but it was so soft I couldn't make out what she said.

I stooped down to her level, keeping some distance between us just in case. Her eyes locked onto mine and my breath rushed out again. I wanted to talk to her but wasn't sure what to say. Then she began to speak.

Nothing she said made sense. The only thing I could pick out was something about "looking for my seventeen children." She continued rambling. Sensing that she was lost somewhere in her own world, I prayed out loud for a few minutes, then ran back inside to get Tachi.

I'd known Tachi since my first few months in Haiti. She was very wise and often watched my girls. She came outside hesitantly and stood with me. She asked the lady a few questions but got the same incoherent responses. Tachi looked back at me, shrugged, and stepped back as if she didn't feel comfortable getting too close either.

As we stood and watched the young woman and tried to

work out what to do, the woman opened a tiny bag and pulled out a crumpled bedsheet. She began opening up the sheet and spreading it out on the concrete driveway in front of the gate.

"What are you doing?" I asked.

The woman ignored us, babbling as she tangled with the sheet.

I stepped forward. "I am sorry but you cannot sleep outside here," I said in a loud voice.

Her posture changed. She straightened up and looked at me with an unmistakable flash of evil in her eyes. A rancid croak came out of her mouth. "The head horseman sent me here. He said if I sleep outside of this gate, he will give me that house." She turned and pointed toward the house across the street.

I turned and looked at the house. *Now why in the world would she want that house?* I thought. Then I took a deep breath and made the connection. *Oh! That's the house we are about to rent for Dan and Rita.*

Rita was the curly-haired woman from Colorado whom I'd met at Son of God Orphanage when the medical team was visiting. She'd shared my concerns about Pastor Joe and what was going on at the orphanage, and we'd become friends and stayed in close touch. One day I sent an e-mail to her, and we began talking about her coming to Gressier to help with the school more often.

I didn't know when I sent the e-mail, her life had been turned upside down. Rita Noel was finishing up a successful career as a middle school teacher and looking forward to a full retirement in a few years when, on a whim, she attended a conference about the plight of the hundreds of millions of orphans around the world. She bought a book about orphans and took it home to show her husband, Dan, an electrician.

She started coming to help us in Haiti, spending more and

more time in the country when her schedule allowed. Then, feeling that God was calling her to invest more in the community of Gressier, she had decided to quit her teaching job, right before I called her.

The Noels were getting everything organized to move to the Caribbean to work with us at Respire Haiti. Rita, to help the school, and Dan, to oversee construction. They'd experienced some significant roadblocks to the plans in Colorado, so in my heart of hearts, I half-expected some opposition with this as well.

I hadn't expected it in the form of a poor, helpless woman sprawled out on the ground in front of my gate, however. I repeated again, firmly, "I am sorry, but you cannot sleep outside here."

She laughed, almost a cackle, and repeated again clearly, "The head horseman sent me here, and I am going to sleep here. Then he will give me the house."

There was nothing else to do, so I began praying over her again and walked inside, pulled the gate shut, and called our staff to come gather and pray with me. After a few minutes we sat together on the front steps, and facing the gate, we began lifting our voices in worship of our Lord and in prayer for this poor woman. It seemed to me that Satan was using her body, and she was helpless and defenseless against it all. It seemed such a low ploy of the enemy to use her to try to attack the Noels, even when they hadn't yet arrived in Haiti.

Our prayers grew louder and more confident. We had the sense that the enemy was losing and had already lost. A peace came over me that surpassed all of this chaos, and I knew the battle belonged to God, and it was over.

I opened the gate and went back outside just in time to see the woman picking up her sheet, stuffing it back into her bag, and running away. The team and I continued to worship, praying for her and her spirit. We prayed the same prayer we used every time we sensed an attack from a person—we prayed we would see her again "in the light of day." We asked God to use us to bring light to her and that we would see her during daytime soon.

Sleep that night was just about impossible as I reflected back on the strange events of the day. Finally I relaxed and fell asleep, but in what seemed only minutes later, I heard a familiar voice outside the gate. "Megan? Megan?" the voice called.

I sleepily made my way down the stairs and out to the gate. It was Bernard waving a piece of paper in my face. He was delivering the leasing paperwork for Dan and Rita's house across the way. I told him I'd sign it and get it back to him as soon as possible. I thought about the woman and the head horseman, expecting a stab of fear to strike me, but even though I searched in my spirit for that same feeling of fear, it was not there. I thanked God for His intervention and immediately felt a feeling of comfort, boldness, and protection. Then a thought came into my head—if Satan was desperate enough to physically place someone in front of my gate to stop me from renting the house for Dan and Rita, then he was not only desperate but pathetic. And I could only imagine what huge things the Lord had planned for Dan and Rita in Gressier.

During my time in Haiti, I have experienced many different encounters with evil, including walking up and interrupting full-blown voodoo ceremonies on Bellevue Mountain, confronting and fighting child trafficking, and battling the abusive restavek situation. Prayer and worship are my secret weapons, whether dealing with a voodoo priest, a corrupt pastor running a sham orphanage, or a servant of the head horseman. I am learning to let God fight my battles.

TWENTY-THREE

Freedom House

"He has sent me to proclaim that captives
will be released, that the blind will see,
that the oppressed will be set free."
—Jesus in Luke 4:18 NLT

I heard a soft tap at the gate. I swung the gate open and saw a young girl about my age with a toddler. She looked tired and so did the baby.

"I can't take care of him anymore," she said. "I have two other children, and I just can't do it anymore." She continued, telling me of all her problems finding food, medicine, and a place to live. I knew what was coming next. It had happened to me before and to many other foreigners here, and it always crushes me. My heart was beating so hard I thought she might be able to hear it too. The girl took a deep breath, looked into my eyes, and said, "I thought you could take my baby because you can do a better job."

As I took a second to gather my words and thoughts, I pleaded with God to help me speak truth into her life, to speak confidence into her parenting ability, and to speak opportunity to us both as we worked together to find a next step.

Then I had an idea, so I shared it with the girl. Her face lit up as I offered her a job carrying sand on the mountain to help build our school. "But I don't have anyone to take care of the baby," she said, her smile melting away.

"You can take your baby with you and we will work on a solution," I said.

The next day, as I stood on a scaffold at the school with a paintbrush in my hand, I heard beautiful singing from behind the building. As I peeked through the metal bars over the window, tears filled my eyes. "Look!" I said to Kat, who was visiting me in Haiti again. "That's her!"

I'd just been telling Kat about the young girl who had knocked on my gate the day before. Now we both watched as she walked with a group of ladies carrying five-gallon buckets of dirt on their heads, her daughter sitting in the shade of the tree on Bellevue Mountain. And as she walked and worked, she sang, "Hallelujah, Hallelujah to the King of kings."

Unfortunately it's not at all unusual here in Haiti to have a woman offer to give you her child. It has happened to me so many times I could have numerous houses full of children by now. It is one of the most heart-wrenching experiences I've ever had, and every time it brings me to my knees at the end of the day. I always beg God to keep these families together, protected, and provided for. And I am again reminded why I am here in Gressier, doing what I am doing.

Through Respire Haiti we are able to provide education for children at an extremely low cost (or free, if needed); we are able to encourage parents that they can keep their children and put them in school; we feed the schoolchildren, and on weekends we feed the community's children; and we provide employment for hundreds of local people.

Women like the young girl who knocked on my gate make me fight harder, work longer, and drop to my knees begging God to show me the steps to take to help these women provide for their families. So many women here in Haiti do not want to give up their children. But so many people, Americans especially, come to Haiti thinking that building orphanages is the only solution to this problem. Instead, the reality is Haiti needs businesses, jobs that would allow these women to raise their own children. These women long to be good parents and mothers to their children, but so often they have no way of providing for their children's needs of food, medicine, and education. With so many problems and obstacles, their stories don't always have happy endings.

Not long ago I ran into my house in a hurry and passed a young girl sitting on my front steps. I made it all the way into the kitchen before I stopped dead in my tracks. *Did I just see what I think I saw?* My eyes welled up with tears. I turned around to walk back outside to see her again, and this time I really looked. She was turned sideways and her belly curved out noticeably, resting in her hands.

A million thoughts spun in my mind. *She's so young. Where has she been? Why couldn't I find her in time?* I closed my eyes tight, prayed to keep in the tears, and turned back around to head outside and sit down next to her.

"Where have you been?" I exclaimed. I bent down to hug her, and she held on to me tightly. I brought her inside where I asked her why she wasn't at school this year. "I looked for you," I said. "I asked everyone, but no one knew where you were."

"I was living with family in the next city over," she said.

"How are you doing?"

She shrugged her shoulders. "I just turned fifteen years old."

I pointed to her belly but couldn't seem to put words together to ask a question that made sense. She knew what I was asking, though.

She looked at the ground and wrung her hands. "I'm pregnant."

"Yeah?" I squeaked out, trying not to assume anything.

It was worse than I thought. She had been walking to her house and was attacked. Mouth covered, held down. After it was over, she told a police officer, but nothing was done. Her attacker got away, never to be found and punished for what he'd done.

I squeezed her hands and looked into her eyes. I saw fear, sadness, hurt, and pain pushed down deep.

Rape is so representative of the ugliness of the enemy and the evil of this present world. As I focused on this dark and broken situation, something that always threatens to break me, the Lord immediately reminded me that "we do not wrestle against flesh and blood, but against the rulers, against the authorities, against the cosmic powers over this present darkness, against the spiritual forces of evil in the heavenly places" (Eph. 6:12 ESV).

God reminds me the battle here on earth is full of tragedies, heartache, and brokenness. But it's not our job to fight against this world. Jesus has overcome the world (John 16:33). Instead, my job is to spread the light.

Because some of our students, such as this young girl, face very difficult, compromising, and unsafe situations at times, I kept feeling as though we needed a small safe house for them. While I had the desire and the dream to do this, I was afraid to move forward and wasn't quite sure how to organize or how to fund it. I also wasn't sure how to choose which girls should be in the safe house.

Of course, once I actually stopped worrying about all of the details, God put everything into place. Honestly, He just began organizing it all, and I had no choice but to catch up with Him and listen.

In January 2013, one of our students came to my house after school to talk. This sixteen-year-old girl had been asked to leave her orphanage because she was too old and the director only wanted young, cute children. Not knowing what else to do, she began living with her stepbrother, who worked in Port-au-Prince during the week. She hardly knew him. As she talked, my heart was drawn to her and her situation.

A few weeks later she came back to my house. That moment is seared in my memory, how she looked me in the eye with enough boldness and intelligence to say, "I am not safe." She was afraid but found the courage to speak up, unlike so many other children her age here. That's all it took for me to take the jump. That same day I sent an army of men, both Haitian and American, with her to pick up all of her belongings from where she was staying. Then she moved into the house with our Respire interns. I didn't yet realize that the wheels were turning and God was showing me that the safe house was needed now.

A few days later the next rescue took place when our sweet and sassy friend (and Respire employee), Darlene, discovered her sixteen-year-old sister was a restavek a few towns over. Through Respire, Darlene had begun to understand the bondage that her sister was in. They hadn't seen each other in five years, but the more Darlene found out about her sister's situation, the more she knew she had to do something. Darlene discussed the situation with me with burning tears of passion in her eyes.

Sadly, it was a typical situation for a restavek. Her sister woke up between three and four in the morning, washed the car, made coffee and breakfast, packed the other children's lunches, and walked them to school. Next, she came home and cleaned, washed clothes, cooked, bought food, and did various other errands. Although she was "enrolled" in afternoon school, she never actually had time to go, nor did she have any schoolbooks. Every night she was up until eleven o'clock doing household chores.

As Darlene expressed her concern about her sister, I could feel the Lord working.

"So what do you think we should do?" I asked her, then prayed silently.

"She can't stay in that situation anymore," Darlene said in a spunky, outraged voice. "I have to get her out, even if I rent a house and she lives close to here. I have to get her."

I smiled at Darlene's righteous anger.

"But I want her to go to school. Can she go to your school?" Darlene asked.

"Of course. Go get her and bring her back here no matter what," I answered. "You know we have room!"

It wasn't easy. The people she'd been living with were holding her birth certificate from Darlene so they could keep her sister as a restavek. Darlene hopped on a motorcycle with Tachi and arrived at the house a few towns over. As she argued angrily, the man holding her sister hostage claimed that he needed her sister to stay because his wife was in the United States giving birth to their third child. Hearing this, Darlene was enraged even more and stood her ground fighting for her sister's freedom.

Days later Darlene's sweet sixteen-year-old sister sat on our porch, rocking back and forth on the hammock. She didn't smile. She didn't talk. Just rocked back and forth. She was in utter confusion and shock at the change, I'm sure. And in time, with therapy, love, and Jesus, she began to adjust to her freedom from slavery.

Within another few weeks we had added a fourteen-year-old, and a sixteen-year-old clutching her own small baby, both escaping from difficult circumstances of slavery and abuse. Now that the staff house was nearly full, this was the kick I needed to move forward. I knew these girls needed a safe place, where they could begin to heal, to forgive, and to grow. I searched around the area for potential houses and almost immediately found one on a hill within walking distance. It was cute, an incredible price, and perfect for the girls. I signed the lease, and we moved forward, furnishing and decorating it for the girls and their children. Everything happened so easily and quickly. I know I shouldn't be surprised at how swiftly God moves sometimes, but I still am.

We named it the Freedom House, and the walls are decorated with inspiring and loving verses from Scripture, making it feel comfortable and safe. The Freedom House girls have started school, and some are learning to be mothers at the same time. They have an incredible house mom who guides them, loves them, and teaches them. What the enemy meant for destruction and ashes, God is transforming into something beautiful and free.

TWENTY-FOUR

Theodore's Dream

Never be afraid to trust an unknown
future to a known God.
—Corrie Ten Boom

Haiti is a country of walls. Everyone in Haiti who can afford to live behind a wall does so. More expensive walls are made of concrete block, ten feet high or more, and with coiled razor wire or broken-glass bottles and spikes embedded in the top. Heavy metal rolling gates give access to the house and yard behind the wall.

People who can't afford walls try to put them up anyway, with sticks and plastic and plywood and old pieces of USAID tarps left over from the earthquake relief efforts. Walls and guards are necessary because people who are hungry and desperate will steal whatever they can, whenever they can, from whomever they can.

Theodore, a tall, thin man from Gressier, knows this. One night he awoke to the sound of someone out front, so he got up out of bed and went to check. Theodore saw a man using a machete to cut plantains out of the tree in his carefully tended garden. The plantains were precious, and Theodore had three boys and his wife to feed, so he rushed out to stop the man from stealing his food.

The thief turned on Theodore and swung the machete right at his face. Theodore put up his hand to ward off the blow, and the machete sliced into his hand almost to the bone.

We got word of Theodore's horrendous injury when his teenage son brought his dad to the house and asked us for help. As Josh and I peeled off the dirty bandage on Theodore's hand, we gasped at the same moment—a doctor from a hospital in a neighboring city had worked on the injury, but it looked as if a butcher had tried to sew together a piece of meat with a few haphazard stitches. The hand didn't seem to be healing, and now Theodore was experiencing a lot of pain, with his fingers and wrist not working well.

"I need my hands to work. How can I farm if I can't use my hands?" We could see the sadness, anger, and fear in Theodore's eyes as he worried about feeding his family. I didn't know how to answer him. All we could do was clean the wound and bandage it back up.

While I was working on his hand, Theodore said something that set off every warning bell I possessed. He was thinking about sending his three boys, between the ages of six and fourteen, to work in the Dominican Republic. He'd heard rumors about the poor treatment of Haitian children there but claimed he had "family." With his injury, he explained quietly, he thought it was his only option.

Then Theodore said something that horrified me even more. A man had come to him once and offered to help. All he needed Theodore to do was bring his children to Port-au-Prince. When

Theodore arrived, the man introduced his children to a stranger. Pointing to Theodore, he said, "This is just a nice man who is helping these children who have no mother and no father." Theodore realized that his children were about to be sold to this stranger, and he grabbed them and left.

After hearing these stories, I begged Theodore to please not do anything with the children right away. "Give me a few days to pray and see what we can do," I asked, finishing up the bandage. He agreed, and I sent him away with a small bag of beans and rice, enough to feed his family for a few meals.

Josh and I talked about Theodore for the next few days. *Where can Respire Haiti use him?* The wall around campus wasn't quite finished, and we needed an extra guard. Theodore would be perfect for the job! We were in the middle of a break from school, so he would have time to heal up.

However, Theodore's pain got worse, and over the next few weeks he continued to lose function in his fingers and wrist. He showed up one day with no feeling in the injured part of his hand and complaining of intense pain. Josh had been praying for this man and had grown to really care about him, so he decided to take him back to the hospital and find a different doctor to look at him. Ten hours later the two returned. Theodore had some green marks on his palm, where they had tested for "feeling," and that was it. No recommendation, no information, and no treatment. Nothing.

It had now been three weeks since we had met Theodore and started helping him with cleaning and bandaging his wound. We knew we needed to do something more, or he could lose all function in his hand. But before we could, Theodore showed up one morning looking a little different, a little happier. He started talking to Josh and told him about a dream he'd had just the night before.

Josh and a group of Americans had surrounded Theodore and prayed for him in a language he didn't know. Theodore was frightened, and he'd looked up at Josh. "What is happening?" he asked.

"We are praying for you," said Josh, calmly.

Theodore was still frightened and anxious as the group prayed in English over him.

Josh said, "You will be healed. You will be delivered. You will not need surgery or to spend any more money on your hand."

Then Josh put some cream on the wound and covered it back up.

The funny thing is that this was all just a dream. None of us had gathered in a group and prayed over Theodore's hand. Josh had not said those words to him or put any medicine on his hand.

But when Theodore woke up from the dream, it had been so real he shook his wife awake so he could tell her about it. As it happens, she had accepted Christ just three days earlier in their local church. She sat up and asked Theodore to move his hand. A little afraid, he slowly lifted his hand and tried to curl his fingers down toward his palm. Then he bent his hand up and down at the wrist and started wiggling his fingers. He couldn't believe it—everything worked, and he could feel all of his fingers. He looked at his wife in amazement. His dream had come true, and he was healed.

As he explained this story to Josh that morning, Josh couldn't believe it either, but he was completely enthralled. He'd never been a part of anything like this before.

Josh has a strong relationship with the Lord, trusts His leading, and has experienced answers to prayer. But he had never witnessed a miraculous, instant healing like the healing of Theodore's mangled hand, with a strange and unusual dream featuring himself thrown into the mix.

When Josh told me about Theodore's dream and his healing, we both were ecstatic. But he was also feeling a little guilty, a conviction that we had *not* actually gathered around Theodore and prayed for healing. He had only dreamed that we did.

So Josh and I, along with the Respire staff, sensed that we needed to pay attention and that God might be teaching us something through Theodore. To honor the vision that God had given Theodore, we decided to meet at six o'clock that night to pray. I was supposed to invite Theodore to come and be there so we could actually pray for him. However, the plan wasn't working because I couldn't reach Theodore. His cell phone was turned off. I tried and tried but couldn't get him.

At six o'clock we gathered on the front steps of the Respire guesthouse to pray. Without Theodore. I suggested we start anyway, hoping Theodore would somehow feel our prayers.

Josh told Theodore's story, explaining in detail the injury, the aftermath, the dream, and the healing. We drank it in and sat in awe at the power of our God. As Josh bent his head to pray for Theodore, we heard someone knocking on the gate. *Bam. Bam. Bam.* The hollow metallic sound resonated through the yard. I ran to open the gate and was shocked to see Theodore. I almost couldn't believe it was him, as if he'd somehow materialized out of thin air.

Theodore came inside with one of his sons, smiled, and began to tell his story. Then we sat him in a chair, and the members of Respire Haiti surrounded him, along with his beautiful child, laid hands on him and his precious son, and began to pray.

We lifted up our voices in a mix of English and Creole, and the beauty of the prayers brought tears to my eyes.

Patrick, one of our incredible staff members, asked Theodore if he wanted to declare his faith. Theodore nodded and smiled with excitement. In front of all of us, he prayed to accept Jesus as his Savior and Lord.

Theodore's dream came true, and now he follows Jesus with all his heart. My faith was strengthened, and my prayer life was changed. Josh told me Theodore's miracle changed his faith completely. We both know we serve a God of miracles both large and small.

A Day in the Life

No place I would rather be
Than here in Your love.
—Will Reagan, "Set a Fire"

As we hustle about in the morning, the smell of Josh's hot coffee fills the air. I look over on the counter next to the coffeepot to see my fresh iced coffee, only there's no ice because we never have any, but it's semi-cold and ready for me to grab. One of the many gifts Josh gives me is this kick start to my morning with the encouragement of coffee.

I bounce in and out of rooms, buttoning shirts, searching for socks, and puffing out little Jessi's 'fro. As the kids finish dressing, they grab their book sacks and head for the stairs.

I hold open the door as, one by one, Michaëlle, Jessica, Saintil, and Johanne give Josh and me kisses, calling out, "Bye, Mom! Bye, Dad!" as they rush down the stairs to walk up to Respire Haiti Christian School on Bellevue Mountain.

Our morning routine is pretty much the only thing that is *normal* about our days here in Gressier. Sometimes I miss the smell of pine trees in Louisiana. I crave Louisiana strawberries and crawfish, and I miss being able to wear even a light sweater. I think about my incredible Louisiana family and their Sunday lunches together. My heart pauses in those moments to reminisce but only for a second. Because when I snap back into the present, I remember that there is no place I would rather be than with my husband and my children in Gressier.

Only minutes after my children head out to school with some of the girls from Freedom House, escorted by our incredible friend Wilbur, do the knocks on the gate begin, and they continue throughout the day.

Bam. Bam. Bam! All day, a series of hollow metallic bangs, repeated as many times as necessary and echoing through the front yard, is accompanied by a loud, "May-ghan . . . May-ghan!" The bangs and calls continue until someone goes down and rolls back the gate to see who's there and what the need is.

It might be a parent who wants to enroll a child in the school but can't pay. Or it might be a child—even small children come to the gate to enroll themselves. Kids often come by for help with homework or tutoring or to use the Internet for research. Moms come by to ask for advice on parenting, relationship issues, and medical problems they and their families have. Job seekers come by to drop off résumés or apply for work at the medical clinic or the school; we have stacks and stacks of résumés.

The hungry come by to ask for food or encouragement or prayer. Injured adults and children come by for help with cuts, bites, sprains and strains, fevers, rashes, and every other first-aid issue you can imagine, including injuries from beatings and whippings. We even deal with animal issues, such as pig bites or bites from free-roaming, rabid dogs. The knocks at the gate never stop; visiting teams always mention the constant knocks, but for me they're so interwoven into the background of Haitian life that they are part of the rhythm of every single day.

My mornings are filled with meetings about a range of topics, from children who are not enrolled in school, to students who are sick, to approving construction projects.

Many mornings after my children leave and the day has begun, I walk over to Respire Haiti Café. As I jokingly say, one of the most difficult things to live without here in Haiti is iced coffee, so when we saw a deserted building on the main road in Gressier, we decided to open a café that would run from early mornings to midday. Tachi, who has truly become one of my closest friends, runs this amazing café. Her love for cooking is contagious and she makes the best iced coffee, *with* ice in it.

Located in Gressier on the national highway, the café hosts a continuous stream of visitors who stop by for hot, homemade cinnamon rolls, fresh-squeezed juice, smoothies, and more. The best part is that it serves as Respire Haiti's office and all the profit goes back to Respire Haiti Christian School.

The vision that God has for Respire Haiti continues to grow. God is moving in Gressier, and He is moving fast. In two and a half years of building, we have more than fourteen classrooms with five hundred students in our school. Our kitchen, storage room, bathrooms, and office for our school are situated on Respire Haiti Christian School's campus. Our medical clinic is adjacent to our school. Josh's desire and love for sports is being put to good use; he has started six competitive soccer teams, and recently started programs for basketball, volleyball, and tennis as well. We have English, reading, art, and other classes in addition to our original Saturday feeding program. Our mission of encouraging, empowering, and educating restaveks, orphans, and vulnerable children is changing lives.

Sometimes people are surprised when they hear the story of Respire, and I get all sorts of questions and comments and suggestions. But there is one response that I will never view as a compliment; it frustrates me when I hear it: "I could never do what you do."

My response is always the same. "Don't we serve the same God? And doesn't He give us all the courage, strength, and boldness we need to do His work?"

Of course we do. And of course He does.

I didn't have a huge plan that was mapped out before I moved to Haiti. God led me to His heart and ultimately to my passion, fighting for freedom and the right to an education for the children of Haiti.

I have seen repeatedly that one of the enemy's biggest forms of oppression here in Haiti is a broken education system. And that is why more and better education really equals freedom.

The key to the future for Haiti is education, and if these kids don't go to school, they won't learn how to read, write, spell, or add. Without these skills they will never be able to start and run businesses or find jobs that can provide for their own families. Some of these kids belong to families that are too poor to send them to school, but many more are just like Michaëlle—orphans with no one who will invest in them or give them a chance. And that is where we come into the picture. As the body of Christ, it's our responsibility to fight for these children. God has called you and me to fight for them.

Although we can never be sure what God's plans are for the future of Respire, at the moment we are planning to add more classrooms to our school as well as to build a community center that connects to our campus. We would love to continue to reach out to even more children through Christ-centered activities such as art, music, dance, and English. Our desire is to one day build a library for the community here too.

Respire Haiti loves working in Gressier, but we also recognize we are not here to save anyone; only Christ can do that. We're here to show these incredible people Jesus and to see Jesus in them; we have just as much to learn from the Haitians' faith as they do from ours. I am encouraged daily by our teachers, staff, and neighbors and their faith in God's provision.

As each day of chaos, joy, and sadness draws to a close, I like to lie on the floor of my girls' room, prop my feet on the wood of Jessica's bed, and stare at the ceiling. Adoption is a beautiful, hard, and (in Haiti) incredibly tricky and long endeavor. There are so many roadblocks, but all I have to do is take one look at my precious children, and I am reminded it's all worth it.

As I rest on the cool tile, I listen to their sweet voices take turns praying.

"Thank You for food."

"Thank You for Mommy."

"Thank You for Daddy."

Then I trail off into my own thoughts about the transformations I have seen, from biting, scratching, and yelling to kissing, hugging, and whispering sweet prayers. I think to myself, *This is redemption, this is beauty, and this is the miracle.*

Notes

Chapter 1: Okay, God, I'm Here

1. *Voodoo* is more often spelled *vodou* in Haitian culture and refers to more than just a religion but an experience that ties both body and soul together.
2. Justin Podur and William I. Robinson, "The Earthquake and Haiti's Politics, 2010/11," in *Haiti's New Dictatorship: The Coup, the Earthquake and the UN Occupation* (London: Pluto Press, 2012), 140.

Chapter 5: A *Restavek*

1. "UN Human Rights Expert Condemns Child 'Slavery' in Haiti," UN News Center, June 10, 2009, http://www.un.org/apps/news/story.asp?NewsID=31089&Cr=slavery&Cr1#.U6nx2RaT7gI.
2. Jean-Robert Cadet, *Restavec: From Haitian Slave Child to Middle-Class American* (Austin: University of Texas Press, 1998), 4.

Chapter 8: The Boy in the Pink Shirt

1. www.behindthename.com.
2. Emma Wilkinson, "Haiti Children Face Ongoing Disease and Trauma," BBC World News, January 15, 2010, http://news.bbc.co.uk/2/hi/health/8461064.stm.

Chapter 9: A Dream Born Under the Tree

1. National Research Council, *Lost Crops of Africa: Volume III: Fruits* (Washington, DC: National Academies Press, 2008), 149.

Chapter 16: A Warning from the First Lady

1. The petition is now closed: https://www.change.org/petitions /ambassador-of-the-republic-of-haiti-close-the-son-of-god -orphanage-and-investigate-ibesr.

Chapter 20: Josh Has Something to Say

1. Will Reagan and United Pursuit, vocal performance of "Take Back," on *Endless Years*, 2012, compact disc.

About the Author

M egan Boudreaux founded the nonprofit Respire Haiti to fight for the freedom of Haiti's estimated 300,000 child slaves. Megan, at the age of twenty-four, followed God's call to begin a feeding program and transform a barren hillside into a refuge and school for five hundred children. Respire Haiti also has a sports complex and kitchen, where two meals a day are served. A medical clinic is nearing completion with future plans for a church, community center, and library.

In 2012, Megan adopted two Haitian sisters. The following year she married her best friend, Josh Anderson, and together they have begun the adoption of another set of siblings.

To learn more about Megan and Respire Haiti, please visit http://respirehaiti.org.